Redfield Proctor & the Division of Rutland

Redfield Proctor & the Division of Rutland

Linda Goodspeed

THE History PRESS

Published by The History Press
Charleston, SC 29403
www.historypress.net

First published 2011

Manufactured in the United States

ISBN 978.1.60949.241.0

Library of Congress Cataloging-in-Publication Data
Goodspeed, Linda.
Redfield Proctor and the division of Rutland / Linda Goodspeed.
p. cm.
ISBN 978-1-60949-241-0
1. Proctor, Redfield, 1831-1908. 2. Rutland (Vt.)--History. 3. Rutland (Vt.)--Biography. I. Title.

F59.R9G66 2011
974.3'7--dc22

Notice: The information in this book is offered without guarantee on the part of the author or The History Press. The author and The History Press disclaim all liability in connection with the use of this book.

For my daughter, Masha, who has brought so much joy and happiness—and fun—into my life. You are an inspiration. Love, Mom.

Portrait of Redfield Proctor by Robert Gordon Hardie, 1892. *From the U.S. Military archives.*

It is an old proverb that money is power. In the marble business, I reversed this and thought power would be money and it proved so. We developed and gave our neighbors such formidable competition we made ourselves and our business felt as a power. We worked for this more than we did mere profit.
—Redfield Proctor

A view of the front of the U.S. Supreme Court, one of the most beautiful buildings in Washington, D.C., highlighting the marble columns. Marble for the building came from the Vermont Marble Company. *iStock Photo.*

Contents

Preface 11

1. Waiting 13
2. Meeting 21
3. Civil War 24
4. Sutherland Falls 34
5. Library 46
6. Office 54
7. Quarry 60
8. Testimony 73
9. Facts 79
10. Dorrs 83
11. W.Y.W. 88
12. Bribe 91
13. Motive 99
14. Mill 111
15. Plan 118
16. Tactics 131
17. Debate 134
18. Final 142

Epilogue 157
About the Author 159

PREFACE

Redfield Proctor and the Division of Rutland is a work of fiction based on the events surrounding the division of Rutland, Vermont, in 1886.

I first became interested in Redfield Proctor and his life and times nearly a quarter century ago while working on a book about the history of Pico, Vermont, and the development of alpine skiing in the United States. Pico is one of the oldest ski resorts in the country.

While researching that book, I learned that Redfield Proctor had once owned Pico, which he used as a private hunting and fishing preserve. Proctor later gave the mountain to his grandson, Mortimer Proctor, as a kind of "coming of age" gift when Mortimer turned eighteen. It was a wonderful story.

Later, after finishing the Pico book, I learned that Redfield Proctor's personal papers had been catalogued and donated to the Proctor Town Library. I was intrigued and started reading through some of them. They were fascinating. I soon narrowed my focus to the events surrounding the division of Rutland, primarily because it was so contentious and so well documented.

In addition to Proctor's own references in his papers to the division struggle, I read several other sources, including newspaper accounts of the day, Vermont histories and other sources. I was a fixture at many libraries, including the Proctor Town Library, the Rutland Free Library, the Castleton State College Library and the Boston Public Library.

The book is based on the historical record of Proctor's life and the division struggle. All of the testimony in opposition to division is what was actually reported. Also, many of Redfield Proctor's own words in the book regarding division, as well as various letters, references to politics, marbling, the business, hunting, fishing and his humor, are taken from his papers.

Upon this historical record I have laid a drama. The drama is comprised of real people from the period, and like any drama, people filled with strong emotions, passions, lusts, doubts and weaknesses. The drama is fictionalized. Many of the characterizations and descriptions (Fletcher's weak character, Frank's poetic sensitivity, Dorr's bluster, etc.), relationships (Proctor's romantic involvement with Mary Myers), as well as some events in the book (Smedburg's blackmail attempt), are my own inventions.

Besides the many helpful librarians who assisted me in my research, there are several other people I want to thank for their support, advice and encouragement during this long project. The folks at The History Press, particularly my editor, Whitney Tarella, did an outstanding job. This book is one of their first forays into historical fiction. Thanks for making me the first.

I also want to thank Kathy VandenBerghe for her sharp eyes during the proofreading and editing stages. Thanks also to Sally Ebeling of Boston, who read an early draft of the book. My webmaster and daughter, Masha, to whom this book is dedicated, deserves a special thank-you for her computer skills and all-around help and support.

And finally, I want to thank my longtime friend, Nancy Parenteau, who I first met in college, for her assistance in gathering the photos for this book and for her encouragement every step of the way. Nancy is a valued friend. We have many shared memories and experiences.

Chapter 1

WAITING

Fletcher Proctor slapped Frank hard on the shoulder.

"Where is my father?" he demanded.

Frank Partridge looked up. Blinking his eyes, he tried to remember where he was. The large, high-ceilinged room echoed with the voices of men, trampling feet and the scrape of chairs and furniture. On the table in front of Frank—usually so neat—papers and books were strewn about. Frank struggled to bring himself back to that room. He flushed at the thought that Fletcher had seen what he was reading and tried to slide his left arm over the thin volume on the table in front of him. Fletcher's large, beefy hand was still on his shoulder, and Frank shrank under it. If Fletcher saw the book or its title, *Sonnets from the Portuguese*, Frank would never hear the end of it. Frank had already read many of the forty-four love sonnets Elizabeth Barrett Browning had written to her husband, but he had long coveted the whole collection. Browning was his favorite poet, and ever since he found the Portuguese collection the week before in the back bins of a book shop in Boston, the volume had not left his side. Now he was sure Fletcher had seen it, too. He braced for the ridicule he knew was coming.

But Fletcher Proctor was too angry and upset to notice what Frank was reading. He stood over Frank, his bloodshot eyes darting around the room. He had come in the side door of the hall behind the table where Frank and the members of the legislative committee sat and so had escaped Frank's notice. His face was flushed with the cold and his breath smelled of onions and tobacco.

"Where is Father?" Fletcher demanded again, still searching the room. "Why hasn't the hearing started? It was supposed to start five hours ago. I've got people to see."

And whiskey to drink, Frank thought.

"Calm down," Frank said, his composure quickly returning once he realized that Fletcher had not caught him reading his poetry volume after all. With a jerk, he shrugged Fletcher's hand off his shoulder and reached for his pen. He slid the top off, dipped it into an ink bottle and, with his head bent low, made a deliberate notation in his notepad to conceal the disgust he always felt in Fletcher's presence. He silently rebuked himself for allowing Fletcher to intimidate him, for being afraid of his scorn and ridicule. He longed now to bring Browning's book out again right in front of Fletcher and ever-so-casually open it and return to his reading. Instead, he made another notation in his notepad.

"He's right over there," Frank said without looking up, "talking to Clement and Dorr and the others."

Fletcher followed Frank's barely perceptible nod toward a group of well-dressed men at the back of the hall.

"Damn!" Fletcher hissed, spotting the back of his father. "Why's he talking to Clement? Didn't he read the editorial in the *Herald* this morning? And Dorr! Is he crazy? Doesn't he know Dorr's going to address the committee against the division proposal?"

"He has his reasons," Frank replied evenly.

Secretly, Frank Partridge was as puzzled as Fletcher at the elder Proctor's behavior. Frank had clipped the editorial that Fletcher had referred to from this morning's *Rutland Herald* and had it with him. He knew Proctor had seen it, too, because Frank had left a copy of it on top of the day's correspondence and newspapers that he always left on Proctor's desk each morning. On the top of the editorial Frank had scrawled, "Percy's revenge."

Frank pulled the editorial from his breast pocket and glanced at it again. It was dated "October 22, 1886."

Frank read quickly: "This proposal to divide the town of Rutland into three towns has been advanced with great skill by ex-Governor Redfield Proctor, who wishes merely to perpetuate his own name and control his own taxation. It is folly and has no support among the people. It is proposed merely for ex-Governor Proctor's own political gain. No man should have so much control and power over the lives of so many others."

Frank refolded the newspaper clip and looked again at Redfield Proctor bantering easily with the father of the author of the editorial. He wondered what the other men in the hall thought of the scene in front of them, or if they were even aware of the fierce political and social jockeying taking place for their benefit. As he surveyed the room, Frank was surprised at how many men were actually still there, at least two hundred, Frank estimated. He knew they must have taken the day off from work to attend the hearing that was being held on a weekday for just that reason.

Damn that Sundqvist! Frank thought as he spied the Swedish giant at the center of a group of men. Frank knew without needing anyone to tell him that Josef Sundqvist was the main reason so many men remained in the room, still waiting. Sundqvist had been nothing but trouble ever since arriving at the mill. Frank wrote the name "Sundqvist" in his notepad and underlined it three times. Frank strained hard to recognize any more men from the company but, except for Sundqvist, couldn't. Not surprising really. Even though Frank spent many hours each day on the quarry floors and in the mills, ever-present notepad in hand, the workers all looked alike to him—big, sweating, grunting, thick-muscled, ignorant beasts. Fletcher called them "work horses," and for once, Frank agreed with him. He gave up trying to recognize any of them and made another note to himself to check the day's attendance records with the foremen. He gazed again at the half dozen well-dressed men at the back of the hall that Redfield Proctor was regaling.

At the head of the group, his back to the table at the front of the hall where Frank and now Fletcher sat, was the oldest of the men. From his age, white hair, bearing presence and the deference the others showed him, Charles Clement was obviously the unofficial leader of the group. It was a position he assumed naturally, without question, as if his by birthright. And in a way it was. Clement was one of Rutland's oldest and most prosperous residents, the president of the Rutland Railroad Company and of two of the town's largest banks, the Clement National Bank and the State Trust Company. Clement knew everybody's business, and nobody did business in the town without, first, his knowledge; second, his approval; and third, his assistance. His son, Percival W. Clement ("P.W." to his workers; "Percy" to the rest of the community), owned the *Rutland Herald*, the town's daily newspaper. At one time, Redfield and Percy Clement had been partners in the newspaper; now they were bitter enemies. Frank had not realized just how bitter until he read Percy's editorial in this morning's *Herald*.

To Charles Clement's left was old Dr. Woodhouse, a short, balding, slightly stooped man of about seventy. Across from him were Judges Nicholson and Dunton and Colonel Gaskill. Seneca Dorr, a large, heavy-set, explosive man with long, flowing white hair brushed back from his broad flat forehead, stood opposite Clement, rounding out the circle. Redfield Proctor had seen the group immediately upon entering the hall. Without any hesitation, as if he had planned it before entering, he strode over to them, placing his hand on Nicholson's shoulder, greeting each by name.

"It's good to see you, Dr. Woodhouse. Sorry to hear about your gout, but you're looking fit now. It's all owing to a Republican administration, I assure you. Seneca, well now, how is the loyal opposition? After that defeat the Democratic Party suffered at the polls last spring, I would think you'd still be home licking your wounds. Charles, you look terrific. What is your secret? I'm very grateful to you all for coming out on such a ghastly day to show your support for our position."

Proctor turned to Dorr and back to Clement with a pleasant smile.

"Redfield, you know we're not here to support you," Clement said sourly. "I've lived in Rutland for thirty-eight years, and as long as I'm alive, I shall never support you or anyone else who would tear this town apart. There's not a town anywhere that's ever been built up by being divided. As long as I'm alive this town will never be divided."

"Charles, be reasonable," Proctor replied. "We can't sit around another thirty-eight years waiting for you to kick the bucket so we can finally bring some orderly government to this town. Rutland's much too large now to be governed properly any longer under town government. Why, the town hall won't even hold all the citizens on Town Meeting Day. What kind of democracy is that? Most of the working-class men in this town are immigrants. They can learn the duties and responsibilities of American citizenship much better in three smaller towns where their votes and opinions count for something rather than in one large town where they can't even participate in their government because the town hall isn't big enough to hold them all. Seneca can tell you the importance of involving the working class in their own government. It's been a personal crusade of his, ever since he got out of the marble business."

Dorr glared at Proctor. "I'd rather warn them about the dangers of creating a political boss who buys votes with jobs."

Proctor put his head back and laughed pleasantly. "Come, come. Let's not use up all of our best rhetoric before the next election. Right now, my main concern is getting this meeting underway. I understand these men have been waiting for several hours."

Proctor turned to leave, thought of something and turned back to Clement.

"Charles, be sure to give mine and Emily's best to Mrs. Clement and, of course, to Percy, dear boy."

Proctor left them quickly, glancing at his timepiece as he strode briskly to the table opposite where Frank and Fletcher sat.

He never stops ticking, Frank thought as he watched Proctor. *Never stops planning or calculating.* Every time Frank thought he had Proctor figured out, Proctor would turn around and surprise him—like today. Frank had been certain Proctor would ignore Clement and the others. Instead, he greeted them like long-lost supporters. There had to be a motive behind the big show of friendship. Proctor did nothing by happenstance. *Probably just to needle Clement,* Frank decided at last. *That and to show the working-class men in the hall that, even alone, Proctor was the equal socially and politically to the whole group of their high-class champions.*

Physically, Redfield Proctor hardly seemed the equal of anyone. He was a short, fairly thin, almost frail-looking man. Acquaintances were always surprised upon meeting him for the first time at just how slight a man he really was. They wondered why they had thought him a much bigger man, how such a compact frame could contain so much force, so much confidence. He had a long, narrow face marked by high cheekbones and a thin, aquiline nose. His eyes were his most prominent feature—widely spaced, cold, hard darts of steel that could flash between kindly, warm humor and cool resolve instantly and without warning. He had heavy brows and a high forehead. He wore a neatly trimmed beard his whole adult life. As a young man, he had brown hair streaked with reddish highlights that now, in middle age, was flecked with gray. He dressed impeccably in expensive tailored clothes that were conservative in cut and taste but unmistakable in their quality. Purpose emanated from his every feature and movement. Even his charm, which was considerable, was purposeful. Time was everything to him. Frank glanced at his own timepiece. He wrote 3:05 on his notepad. The meeting was now more than five hours late in starting. *Exactly on schedule,* Frank thought.

The meeting was the second of three public hearings on the proposal to divide the town of Rutland, Vermont, into three smaller towns. It was mid-October 1886, and already snow could be seen on the mountains to the east. The hearing had been scheduled to start at 10:00 a.m. Shortly before the prewarned time, a small group of men began gathering outside the feed store in West Rutland where the hearing was to take place in one of the store's large back rooms. The men waited patiently, thirty minutes, an hour. Finally, a short, thin man with a thick, drooping mustache appeared from inside the building. He looked nervous and kept pulling on his mustache. The meeting will be late in starting, he told the men. Some of the members of the committee had been delayed in arriving by the snow.

The men shouted to be let inside to wait, but the messenger slipped quickly back inside the door.

"There's no snow on the roads!"

"The roads are fine! Let us in!"

The men were jostling each other and getting angry. They began arguing among themselves.

"The committee members didn't have to travel! They spent the night here."

"That's right!" More pushing. "They stayed in town last night!"

"They stayed at Governor Proctor's house," a young man broke in. "I saw them turn into his drive about 7:00 p.m. last night after the hearing in Proctor."

The men were hungry and cold. Most were small merchants or laborers who had had to close their shops or take the morning off from work. It was now past lunchtime, and they had not eaten. Most stood in the chilling wind without hats or gloves. Soundlessly, one after another slipped away—hungry, cold, frustrated. Only Sundqvist—sinewy, deeply tanned arms bare in a thin, open-necked, cotton shirt—seemed oblivious to the cold or the wait. He was one of a half-dozen quarrymen from Proctor's marble company at the hearing. He talked easily and constantly, making the rounds from one to another, keeping his own little band together and rallying the others. Smiling, earnest, confident, he urged them to stay, to stick it out.

"Ve *must* stay," he told them. "It von't be long now. Ve *must* stay."

Finally, a few minutes after 2:00 p.m., the doors opened and the men, the ones who remained, numbed in body and spirit, were allowed to enter. Still, they waited. Finally, just before 3:00 p.m., Proctor entered the room. A few minutes later, the committee members came in.

As Proctor took his seat at the other end of the table from him, Frank caught his eye and nodded, smiling slightly. He opened a clean page in his notepad and turned his attention to the center of the table where the speaker of the Vermont House of Representatives was getting ready to address the gathering.

Judge Luke P. Poland disliked a large fuss. Despite his public position, he was a private man who preferred to work behind the scenes, quietly and out of the glare of the public eye. In all of his long political career in the Vermont legislature and on the bench, he had never been involved in such a hotly debated or contentious issue. He read the *Herald* regularly and could not believe the venom this division issue had generated. The War Between the States had been over for more than twenty years, but one would never know it from the climate in Rutland. The proposal to divide the town had pitted the masses against their masters in a fashion that Poland found almost frightening. Reading the *Herald* and listening to the testimony at these public hearings, Poland was stunned by the force of the attacks against not only ex-governor Proctor's proposal but against Proctor himself. There were, of course, the middle-of-the-night anonymous acts of vandalism and protests, but the public daylight raids were what surprised the speaker. Signing petitions and letters to the editor of the daily newspaper in big bold letters seemed to Poland a risky business. Attending hearings and speaking out, not only against the proposal but also against the man himself, struck Poland as downright suicidal. In his wildest dreams, no matter how brazen the proposal might be—and Poland had seldom seen such brazenness as this, even in the rough and tumble of Montpelier—he would never have predicted such a public outcry against the richest and most powerful man in the state. And here he was, right smack dab in the middle of it.

Poland sighed heavily as he stood and slowly gaveled the meeting to order.

"This hearing shall come to order for the purpose of hearing testimony on the proposed charter that has been brought before the legislature of the State of Vermont by citizens of the town of Rutland."

A hearing to hear testimony. Great observation, Poland thought, cursing himself at his choice of words. He put on his glasses and picked up a stack of papers from the table, searching desperately for someone else's words to help him out. He read: "Shall the Town of Rutland be divided into thirds for the purpose of granting additional town charters to the villages of Proctor and West Rutland…"

"No!" interrupted a voice from the back of the hall.

The men in the room, listless a moment ago, suddenly came to life. A buzz swept the hall.

"No!" shouted the voice from the back of the hall again.

"Order! Order! I will have order!" Poland pounded the table furiously with his gavel, his face reddening. "I will have order. Order in this room!"

The noise subsided.

"Those who wish to address this committee must identify themselves and be recognized by the chair," Poland said sternly.

"Seneca Dorr, sir," shouted Dorr again, striding to the front of the room. "A resident of the grand old town of Rutland, the largest and most prosperous town in the free and independent state of Vermont. I respectfully request permission to address the members of the legislative committee."

"Harrumph." Poland sat down.

Chapter 2

MEETING

"Honorable members of the committee and fellow citizens of this grand old town of Rutland," Dorr began.

He stood to the left of the committee members near the front of the hall, his head back, feet apart.

"The proposed town of Proctor, one of the three towns that would be created by carving up and dismembering Rutland, is an area of six square miles. It has a transient population almost wholly at the mercy of the Vermont Marble Company, which is really not a Vermont company at all but a New York corporation. The Vermont Marble Company owns all the land that can be utilized in the town, and employs nine of every ten voters who reside in the town.

"This foreign corporation is under the control of one man. This man's control is so complete that the proposed new town even bears his name: Proctor. Imagine that! A man who owns his own town!

"Now, of course, we all know that this man is an honorable man. He is a former governor of our state, a colonel in the bloody conflict that preserved our precious union. But, gentlemen, no man, no matter how honorable a man, should have the kind of power that this man wants! And what will happen if this man should die? Life is not certain for any of us, not even for Governor Proctor! Yes, even Governor Proctor is liable to die one day!"

A titter ran through the crowd. Frank looked at Proctor. No sign. Frank turned back to his notes.

"You know what will happen when Governor Proctor dies?" Dorr raised his voice. "I'll tell you what will happen! The New York Corporation is liable to send some brainless fellow up from the city to manage the affairs of the town, and the people of Proctor will be so unhappy they will petition Rutland to take them back again!"

The men in the audience turned to one another grinning and laughing. A few began clapping. Dorr silenced them with his hand.

"But it will be too late then! Once divided, a house is forever divided. But we don't have to divide this grand old house! We are the largest and the richest town in the state of Vermont! If we don't want to divide we don't have to divide!"

"No! No! No!" a shout went up from the crowd. A few of the men began clapping in unison. Frank could see Sundqvist above the clapping and shouting, egging the others on. He again wrote the name Sundqvist in his notepad.

Dorr continued: "The only argument that has been made in favor of division is that Rutland has become too large for town government and that its town hall is inadequate for its population. But where is the proof that the town is misgoverned? Rutland is one of the best governed towns in the state! Town meetings are always orderly. And over the last ten years, the town debt has been reduced to just over the grand list. The average town tax rate is less than thirty cents! Is that proof of anarchy? Is that proof the town is misgoverned? I tell you, Rutland is the envy of every town in the state!

"And the argument that the town needs to be divided because the town hall is too small is not even worthy of argument. Why divide and build three new town halls when a simple addition to the one we have will do?

"If this petition to divide Rutland passes the legislature, it will mean that every town in the state, as soon as it becomes rich and prosperous, will face the prospect of being carved up and beggered. It will greatly increase the number of small towns in the state and the burdens on local and state expenses. Large towns add to the wealth and resources and character of the state and attract young men, counteracting the serious drain of Vermont youth to cities out of state.

"We should be changing Rutland's government, not its boundaries! The petition before the legislature should be for a city, not for division into even smaller towns!"

More clapping and shouts. Dorr suddenly lowered his voice. "This proposal is nothing more than a contest between the people on the one hand and one man, wealth and corporate greed on the other. It has been conducted by the latter as if the people have no rights. The sentiment against division has been treated with contempt and as not of the slightest consequence by Governor Proctor, who is not content to control the jobs and the wages of his workers!"

Dorr's voice rose to a crescendo. "Now he wants to control their votes as well!

"Well, Governor Proctor," Dorr dramatically paused, turning to face Proctor who was listening intently at the committee table, "I tell you, the votes of the free and independent citizens of the Town of Rutland, Vermont are not for sale! Not to you, not to anyone, not for any price!"

Dorr's face had reddened and his long white hair had fallen over his forehead. "This is one contest you and your New York Corporation are not going to win!"

The men in the hall had fallen silent, stunned by Dorr's direct challenge to Proctor. They had forgotten their cold and their hunger and their long wait. They listened to Dorr as if spellbound. A man actually uttered out loud what they dared not even think. Dorr turned back to them, addressing them almost gently.

"Gentlemen," he told them. "Governor Proctor does not care about your rights or what is good for this town and its citizens."

His voice turned hard. "The only right Governor Proctor cares about is the right of money and the right of power!"

Chapter 3

CIVIL WAR

Colonel. Governor. Secretary of War. Senator. Political Boss. Multimillionaire.

Of all the many titles Redfield Proctor collected during his long life, the one he preferred was the first—the one from his soldiering days in the Civil War.

It was somewhat ironic that he should have such fond memories of army life, having nearly lost his life in the war. But his brush with death was from tuberculosis in a hospital bed far from the front and not from Rebel gunfire. The paralyzing fear and deprivations of battle and long marches were far from Proctor's wartime experiences. He liked to tell of his being at Gettysburg, but in truth, he came no closer than two miles to the fighting. For Proctor, war was not the hell of gunfire and the screams of dying men. War for Proctor was pleasant camaraderie and a lifelong bonding among men that he treasured and carried with him.

For Proctor, the outbreak of hostilities in 1861 could not have come at a more welcome time. At last, he felt galvanized, purposeful. When fighting broke out that spring, Proctor left the Boston law office of his cousin, former Vermont Supreme Court chief justice Isaac F. Redfield, on a day's notice to return to Vermont to enlist. He was thirty years old and had been admitted to the bar for less than a year, but already he disliked being a lawyer. Ten years out of college, he still did not know what he wanted to do with his life. The war at last gave him a sense of purpose.

Redfield Proctor was born on June 1, 1831, in Proctorsville, Vermont, the son of Jabez and Betsey (Parker) Proctor. He came from old Vermont stock, his grandfather having settled the town near Ludlow that eventually took his name. Redfield attended Black River Academy in Ludlow, Vermont, and Danby Academy in Danby, Vermont. He graduated from Dartmouth College in 1851. He spent the next several years wandering aimlessly. He went west to seek his fortune but ended up losing his father's small inheritance on a bad real estate deal in Minnesota. He returned to Vermont penniless and decided to try his hand at running the family farm in Proctorsville for his mother. In 1858, he married Emily Dutton from the neighboring town of Cavendish. The families were not on good terms prior to the marriage. Farming did not suit Proctor, and he decided to try law, entering Albany Law School in 1859. He was admitted to the bar a year later and went to Boston to clerk for his cousin, leaving his wife, Emily, and two small babies on the family farm in Proctorsville. But after only a few weeks in his cousin's drab little office off Milk Street, all Proctor could see ahead of him were dull, dusty law books and a life of drudgery.

The sound of gunfire that split the air on April 12, 1861, when the Confederate army opened fire on the tiny federal outpost at Fort Sumter in the harbor off Charleston, South Carolina, seemed to reverberate loudly through Proctor's empty office. It rattled the walls and interrupted his thoughts with the insistency of a drumbeat. Finally, his concentration shattered and his thoughts flashing to visions of battle and glory, Proctor closed his book, got up from his desk and went to the window. The drum was below him. He threw up the window and felt the excitement and anticipation wash over him like the wind from a rising storm. Below him, a drummer and two men playing fifes marched slowly down the narrow, debris-strewn street crowded with horses, carts and buggies. Several dogs and a pig rooted among the garbage. A man in an army coat stood talking animatedly to a small group of men clustered around him. He blew his nose on his sleeve and continued his excited revelry. Several boys hawked newspapers in the street.

"Rebs open fire on federal troops! Lincoln issues call for seventy-five thousand men! Read all about it! War has begun!"

A clatter of soldiers on horseback rounded the corner and passed under Proctor's window, scattering dogs and passersby. Proctor felt his heart leap.

"What's the word?" he called to one of the young newspaper boys below him when the soldiers had passed.

"Those Johnny Rebs'll be put down in three months!" the boy shouted back, pumping his fist at Proctor.

Three months! Proctor returned to his desk and found a legal pad.

"Dear Cousin," he wrote hurriedly. "The sovereignty of our Union is in peril. Even as I write, the sound of gunfire echoes from the harbor outside Charleston. The very flag our ancestors carried into battle and fought and died for nearly a century ago has been fired upon. Our freedom, our honor, our heritage, everything we hold dear, has been violated. Our very way of life is at stake. We cannot let this act of aggression and treason against our precious nation go unpunished. Our new and able president has called for seventy-five thousand men to join in the defense of our Union. Just as our forefathers answered the call to duty nearly a century ago, I, too, must answer the call of my President. We cannot let the land our fathers fought and died for be torn apart. I leave in the morning for Rutland and will apply for an officer's commission in the Union army. I ask your indulgence and your prayers. I entrust Emily and the children to your benevolence. I know you will understand the duty to country that calls me. Your humble servant and cousin, Redfield Proctor."

Proctor left the pad on his cousin's desk, picked up his hat and shut and locked the door to the law office behind him. He arrived in Proctorsville the next afternoon. With barely a greeting for Emily and the children, he set off to the Union recruiting offices in Rutland.

In June 1861, Proctor received a commission as a lieutenant and regimental quartermaster of the Third Vermont Volunteers and was placed on the staff of General William F. "Baldy" Smith.

Proctor was a bright, eager young man with an officer's commission and a sharp eye for horse flesh that was to serve him well on the general's staff. Since he was a boy, horses had been a special love. His father had died when Proctor was only eight, and his childhood had been hard and lonely. Horses helped fill that void, and he spent many long hours brushing them, talking to them and taking care of them. He was an expert horseman and saw in horses qualities others did not. An acquaintance near his mother's farm in Proctorsville was surprised when Proctor asked him for the weak young foal that had been born a few weeks earlier. The foal was a spindly young colt with exceptionally high withers that gave it an ungainly appearance and gait. He bared his teeth and shook his head furiously as he awkwardly stumbled around the pasture.

"I like that one," Proctor told the farmer, pointing to the awkward young colt.

Proctor was running his mother's farm and had stopped to look at the young horses on his way home. There were several new foals in the pasture.

"That one?" the farmer repeated incredulous, following Proctor's gaze. "It's all out of proportion. Look at the way he runs, legs every which way. He's weak, you can tell. Look at the others his age. They're not as tall as he is, but much better proportioned. He's going to be a mean one, too. Look at the way he shakes his head. You'll never be able to train that one. You'd be better off with one of the others."

"I like him," Proctor repeated, following the young colt with his eyes. "He's going to grow into those legs, you watch. And that's not meanness, that's spirit. He'll be high tempered, no doubt, but he's got the most intelligent face I've ever seen. Look at his withers. He's going to be huge, seventeen hands at least."

The farmer shook his head, watching the colt stumble and fall on his right foreleg. "If you think you can do anything with him, go ahead. He's yours."

Proctor named the colt Traveler. "You and I are going to have some fine travels together," he told the colt softly, stroking his handsome face. Traveler pawed at the ground impatiently and nuzzled Proctor's breast pocket looking for apples.

True to Proctor's prediction, Traveler grew into a beautiful, finely muscled stallion, seventeen and one-half hands high with a brilliant blaze down his face. He had a deep chest with well-muscled haunches. He had enormous stamina, and although high spirited, he seldom frightened. After Proctor enlisted, he rode Traveler into General Smith's camp, where the horse was universally admired and pronounced the finest horse in the Union army. When Proctor learned that General Robert E. Lee's great Civil War mount was also named Traveller (although spelled with two l's instead of one), Proctor was both pleased and proud, good naturedly shrugging off the teasing of his fellow officers.

"It's not a coincidence the best horse on each side is named Traveler," Proctor told the others. "It just means that Lee and I must be the two best horsemen, even if only one of us is a general."

A horse was a man's most important possession in the war, more important even than a gun because horses were so scarce. A horse separated the officers from the enlisted men; generals one from another.

Proctor's eye and his shrewd bartering quickly made him a favorite with senior officers who respected both his advice and his ability to deliver. Within two months and a half-dozen horse trades after his staff appointment to General Smith, Proctor was made a major in the Fifth Vermont Regiment. His horse trading during the war also helped him to complete his first successful business deal. Slowly, he was beginning to find his special niche in the world.

The opportunity, as sometimes happens, came unexpectedly. As Proctor returned to his tent one morning, following the day's briefing with the other senior members of the regiment, a young officer walking in his direction hailed him.

"Redfield, by George, how are you?"

The young man was Colonel Wheelock G. Veazey, commander of the Sixteenth Vermont Regiment, which was bivouacked nearby. Proctor and Veazey had first met at Dartmouth more than ten years before and had immediately struck up a friendship. Veazey hurried over to Proctor and grasped his hand.

"I haven't seen you in a coon's age," Veazey said. "How are you? Staying out of the line of fire, I hope."

Proctor slapped Veazey on the shoulder. "Wheelock, God, it's good to see you. I heard your regiment was in the area. You look great. Army life must agree with you. How long are you camped here? Long enough for me to win back some of that money I lost to you in that last poker game, I hope?"

Veazey laughed. "You never learn, do you? My orders are to report to the commander of the Fifth and wait for instructions from him."

"His tent is over there," Proctor pointed him toward the large tent from which he had just emerged.

"Come get me after you give your report. I'll show you around the camp."

That night Proctor set up a card game in his tent. Veazey brought a young officer from his unit named Adolphus Smedburg. Smedburg, who was Veazey's supply captain, was a small man with a thin, pinched face and sallow, pitted complexion. Proctor instantly disliked him.

"He cheats at cards," Veazey confided quietly to Proctor after Smedburg went outside in the middle of a game to relieve himself, "but I still haven't figured out how he does it."

"He doesn't look like the soldiering type. What's he doing in the army?" Proctor asked quietly, putting down a card.

"His father's furious with him," Veazey replied. "The old man's in the diamond business in New York City. Seems that young Adolphus here was being groomed to take over the family business but got a little too greedy too fast. He bought a shipment of diamonds on the black market and didn't tell his father. The stones were all fakes. When Adolphus couldn't unload them, his old man had to cover the loss. He sent him off to war to punish him."

"Nice father," Proctor said. "What's he doing in the Vermont regiment?"

Veazey laughed. "His father bribed the recruiting officer. If he was going to send his son off to war, the old man at least wanted him someplace where he'd be useful. He figured a supply captain would have plenty of opportunity to do a little freelancing and pocket a profit now and then. Our supply captain was killed when the Rebs ambushed one of our scouting parties near Ball's Bluff in Virginia. The next thing I know the army sends me Smedburg."

"Do you trust him?" Proctor asked quietly, looking inquiringly at Veazey.

"No. I wouldn't trust him as far as I can throw him. But you know," Veazey leaned forward toward Proctor and lowered his voice further, "if I ever needed someone to do some dirty work for me, he's the man I'd turn to."

Just then Smedburg entered the tent, his face ashen in the thin glow of the tent lantern.

"Jeez," he whined in a flat nasal voice, his eyes bloodshot. "This food's gonna kill me."

Two days later, Veazey's regiment was ordered to proceed with the Fifth to the outskirts of Washington. President Lincoln had just recalled General George B. McClellan to Washington and made him general-in-chief of the Union army. McClellan was now organizing a force of 150,000 men, the largest army ever assembled in America. As all the various units in the area began to move out to join McClellan's army, Proctor saw Veazey riding ahead of him. He caught up to him and reined Traveler alongside his friend.

"Do you have any idea what pine tar sells for in Virginia?" Proctor asked.

Just then a wagonload of chickens bumped past them in the mud, startling Veazey's horse. He quickly tried to rein him in.

"No," Veazey said, patting his horse's neck and pulling back on the reins. "Should I?"

As the chickens swayed wildly ahead of them, Veazey's horse settled down, and the two men resumed their conversation.

"Ten cents a barrel," Proctor replied.

"Is that expensive?"

"Expensive!" Proctor exclaimed. "That's less than a tenth what it sells for in Vermont."

"Why this sudden interest in pine tar?" Veazey asked.

"Because it's the best axle grease for wagons."

"I know that," Veazey said. "Every wagon carries a tar bucket and paddle on the rear axle. What's your point?"

Just then, the covered cook wagon bumped by them, piled high with swinging pots and provisions, swaying precariously as it ground through the mud. Both men involuntarily looked at the rear axle as the wagon passed. A bucket, glistening black with sticky tar, swung wildly,

"Why's it so expensive up North?" Veazey asked. "We certainly have enough pine trees."

"You need pitch pines," Proctor said. "Tar and turpentine are distilled from the resin in the knots of the trees. There are pitch pines up North, but nothing like the pine barrens in Virginia down through Georgia."

"And that likely accounts for the price difference, I'm sure," Veazey said impatiently. "Thank you, my friend, for that most uninteresting piece of geography. After the war's over, I propose we go into the pine tar exporting business in Richmond."

"After the war!" Proctor exclaimed. "Are you kidding? Don't you get it? The reason pine tar is so high in Vermont and the other northern states is *because* of the war. The supply from the Southern states has been cut off. After the war, the supply will be reinstated and the price will go down. We should go into the pine tar business now, not after the war."

"Great idea, except you forgot one little detail. Virginia's an enemy state. How do you propose to transport the pine tar out of Virginia back up to Vermont?"

The two men rode slowly through the mud. It had rained again the night before and the road they were traveling was rutted and soft. Carts rumbled by, spraying them with dirty water. Men in uneven columns and dirty uniforms slogged wearily beside them, stumbling and cursing. Pigs, chickens, roosters, dogs and all the other assortment of farm animals that traveled with an army ran crazily through the columns. As far ahead and as far behind as they could see, the road was choked with this flowing humanity.

"What we need is somebody in charge of a supply train," Proctor muttered. He looked sideways at Veazey. Veazey said nothing. Proctor spurred Traveler to the side of the road out of the way of a cannon-loaded cart.

"Let me know if you come up with any ideas," he said as Veazey continued along ahead of him. "I know a sergeant in an outfit a little south of here who'll buy us up all the Virginia pine tar we want. All we have to do is transport it north."

That night, the two Vermont regiments joined other northern troops gathering outside the capital. Unsure how long the encampment might last and not knowing when he might be able to load up again once the troops moved out, Veazey sent Smedburg on a supply run. On the way, Veazey told the nervous little captain to make a quick detour into Rebel territory outside Leesburg, Virginia, to pick up a train load of "urgent war materials."

"General Buell has ordered me to pick up the shipment and transport it north to Baltimore with all speed possible," Veazey lied to Smedburg. "You'll be met in Baltimore by a Major Potter from the War Department. Potter'll take charge of the shipment from that point. My orders are to get that shipment to Baltimore as fast as possible and then load up a shipment of supplies for the trip back."

Operation "Urgent Pine Tar" worked like greased lightning. Using his mother's farm as collateral, Proctor told his sergeant friend to buy him five thousand barrels of Virginia pine tar. For his trouble, the sergeant was promised an exceptional quarter horse. Smedburg met the sergeant at the agreed-upon rendezvous spot five miles outside Leesburg. The "urgent war materials" were quickly transferred onto the Union train and then sped north to Baltimore. At Baltimore, government troops under the direction of Major Potter of the Third Vermont Volunteers, Proctor's old outfit, worked feverishly to unload the materials onto a barge headed north for the Hudson River and then overland by cart to Vermont. No one thought to ask why urgent war materials were needed in Vermont or to inspect what those materials might be. No one, that is, except for a thin, sallow-faced Union supply captain named Adolphus Smedburg.

Following their rendezvous with McClellan's army outside Washington, Proctor and Veazey did not see one another again until after the war. Proctor's regiment participated in the early part of the Peninsula Campaign, the Union's bold plan to capture the peninsula between the James and York Rivers that led to Richmond, the Confederate capital. But in April 1862, Proctor contracted tuberculosis and was ordered home. He did not make it and was confined to an army field hospital, where the surgeons were so convinced he would not survive that they ordered condolences sent to Emily Proctor. Proctor eventually did recover, but the incident cost him his health and his commission. He resigned from the army in July 1862 and returned home to Proctorsville.

Life at home was pale and dull compared to the excitement he had experienced in the army. He quickly grew tired and irritated with Emily's insistent cloying and the crying of the babies.

"Do you like this material better or this one for the curtains in the front room, dear?"

Emily was holding up two swatches of fabric for Proctor to admire. He was sitting in a chair on the front porch trying to read the newspaper, but it was nearly impossible with Emily constantly interrupting him with ridiculous questions about curtains.

"I told you yesterday it does not matter to me," Proctor said impatiently.

"But that was for the drapes in the parlor."

"Parlor, front room—what's the difference? It does not matter to me. Choose whatever one you like best. Just leave me in peace."

The papers were full of a great battle outside Sharpsburg, Maryland, near a little creek called Antietam. Proctor noisily shook the papers and went back to his reading.

"Well—I never." Emily bustled back inside the house. "You don't have to be cross about it."

She was a short, plain-looking woman with little style or shape. Three children had taken their toll on her waist. Proctor heard her speaking to the children in the kitchen.

"Leave your father alone. He's tired today and does not want to be disturbed."

Proctor sighed and put the papers down. He stood up and began pacing the floor.

By the fall of 1862, life at home had sufficiently motivated him to recover his health well enough to accept the colonelcy of the Fifteenth Vermont Regiment. The fact that he was able to recover so quickly from his near fatal brush with tuberculosis was a testament to his determination and will and his great love of the outdoors. Every day he took long walks around his mother's farm, breathing deeply, slowly rebuilding his strength and lungs. In October 1862, less than six months after lying near death in an army field hospital, Proctor began active duty again.

Although the Fifteenth served at the Battle of Gettysburg, the unit did not participate in the actual fighting on Cemetery Ridge. Instead, Proctor and his men spent those hot horrible days guarding the corps trains some two miles from the front. Even from that distance, however, they could still see, hear and feel the awful battle that was taking place.

"I'll never forget how the cannon fire turned the sky red with heat," Proctor would tell audiences years after the war. "Or maybe it was the blood that turned it red. I still wake up in the middle of the night seeing that horrible, blood-red sky. It was a sight, let me tell you. I will never forget it."

After Gettysburg, the Fifteenth returned to Vermont in July 1863, its nine-month tour over. Proctor was mustered out in August, reluctantly, for he had thoroughly enjoyed himself.

It was natural that Proctor, who had been close enough to see and forever remember the horror and awful sights and sounds of battle, but not close enough to actually experience the heat, isolation and fear of close combat, should recall his war service fondly and remember the time as the best years of his life. Except for his bout with tuberculosis, he had never been in any imminent, real danger of losing his life. Even so, he had known the exquisite exhilaration and thrill of living on the edge, the acute adrenalin rush of fear and the tremendous excitement and urgency of war. Army life brought out in him talents and obsessions he had never even known he possessed. He bartered and traded and wheeled and dealed; he politicked. He had never known he could be so shrewd. He absolutely loved the lifestyle of war: camping outdoors, the discipline, the close camaraderie among the men, the pecking order. Even then he had the politician's instincts and the memory of an elephant (he was, of course, a lifelong Republican). He never forgot a face or a name. One of the legends that grew up around him in his own lifetime was his ability to enter any town in Vermont and know at least one man by sight, by name and by regiment from his Civil War days. It was grass-roots politicking at its best, and Proctor continued to cultivate his Civil War contacts and friendships throughout his life. Those contacts formed the basis of what was to become the most powerful political machine in Vermont's history.

Chapter 4

SUTHERLAND FALLS

Redfield Proctor was thirty-four when he won election to his first political office, if heading an organization he formed himself could be called winning office.

In 1865, already nostalgic for his soldiering days and the tight friendships of the men in his regiment, he formed the Reunion Society of Vermont Civil War Officers with himself as its first president. The Reunion Society met every year without fail until Proctor's death in 1908. Proctor never missed a reunion.

He was even older, thirty-eight, before he got his first decent job, and like his first political office, that, too, was inauspicious. In 1869, he arranged with a local judge to have himself appointed receiver of Dorr and Myers, a tiny, debt-riddled marble mill in Sutherland Falls that had never turned a profit.

"Where did the name, 'Sutherland,' come from?" Frank asked Proctor years later.

The two men had just emerged from one of the many mill buildings along Otter Creek and had stopped briefly to take in the sight of the crashing falls with its steep drop. The cascading water and noise of the falls never failed to impress Frank. He was still wearing the large, thick-framed safety glasses the men often donned inside the mill to protect them from flying debris thrown out by the wire cutters. A fine spray of water drops from the falls speckled Frank's glasses as he turned to look at Proctor.

"Apparently some fellow named Peter Southerland," Proctor replied.

"South-erland?" Frank repeated, lowering his head to disentangle the glasses from his face.

"Yes, I guess over the years people started spelling it Sutherland. In the mid-1700s, before Vermont was a state, Southerland moved here from the New York grants. As the first settler, he got naming rights."

Frank chuckled, slipping the glasses into his breast pocket. "Did he start the marbling?"

"No, he was just a farmer. According to some of the mill's ownership papers I read, it wasn't until 1837 when a couple of brothers by the name of Humphrey built the first marble mill in Sutherland Falls. The Humphreys used the falls just as we do today for power to cut and polish the blocks," Proctor said, nodding at the falls.

"So what happened to the Humphreys?" Frank asked.

The two men turned away from the falls and began walking back toward the company offices in the middle of the town, following the railroad tracks that ran alongside them.

"Like everybody else who tried marbling here, they never made any money at it. The biggest problem then was transportation. The railroad hadn't come in yet, and everything had to be transported by horses and oxen. Marble from Sutherland Falls was horse-drawn to Whitehall, New York, thirty miles away, where the blocks were loaded onto barges and floated by canal down to Troy and Albany and then transferred onto steamers down the Hudson. The horse carts would load up with supplies at Whitehall to bring back to Rutland, but it was still a losing proposition."

"When did Dorr come into the picture?"

"Shortly after the war," Proctor replied. "Dorr and John Myers went into partnership and bought the mill together. When John died, Dorr and John's widow, Mary Myers, started fighting. Dorr wanted to sell the mill, but Mary did not."

"It must have been making money," Frank said. "The railroads were here by then."

"You'd think," Proctor shook his head disdainfully, "but the accounts were a shambles. The place was in bankruptcy. I think Dorr's intention was to sell the mill to the Ripleys. They were in the marble business in Center Rutland, and Dorr had married Julia Ripley. Old man Ripley was still alive then. He was pretty shrewd. I'm sure he thought he could pick up the mill pretty cheap. But Mary was determined that that was not going to happen."

Proctor nodded his head at the memory. "She hated Dorr. Good thing," Proctor turned to Frank and smiled. "If it hadn't been for Mary Myers,

Sutherland Falls. The falls were a cheap and plentiful source of power for the Vermont Marble Company. *Dean Goss photo.*

it might have been the Ripleys standing here today instead of us."

He put his arm around Frank's shoulders, and the two men continued back to the offices.

Proctor first met Mary Myers in November 1869. By this time, Proctor had moved Emily and the three children to a farm outside Rutland that he bought with his wartime profits from the pine tar deal. Veazey had used his share to purchase a block on Main Street in downtown Rutland where the two men set up a law partnership called Proctor & Veazey. In the years following the Civil War, Proctor divided his time between farming and practicing law.

Proctor was never cut out to be a lawyer. He hated the confines of the profession.

"There are two ways of practicing law," he once remarked. "One is to search the authorities and evolve out of them principles to apply to the case in hand. And the other is to reason out the principle applicable and then to look for authorities to sustain it. Neither appeals to me."

But the Myers case intrigued him. He was, of course, attracted by the opportunity to lock horns with Dorr, a man Proctor disliked not only for his politics but also for the scorn he had for Dorr's financial dependency on his wife's money. Dorr, alone, would have been enough to lure Proctor into the case. But the presence of Mary Myers brought an element of excitement to the proceedings that Proctor found irresistible.

The day Mary first walked into Proctor's office had been a particularly dissatisfying one. Emily was in bed with another of her bouts of indigestion, and six-year-old Fannie—the third of Proctor's eventual five children—had been up all night with a fever.

"That po'r chil' has her mother's constitution all over," the nanny told Proctor when, alarmed at the child's whimpering and the feel of her burning forehead when he knelt by her bed to stroke her hair, he had sent for the doctor.

Proctor sat in a chair in the upstairs parlor off the hall the rest of the night, dozing fitfully, getting up every few hours to go to Fannie's door and peer quietly at his tiny daughter. The doctor and the nanny dozed in chairs on either side of her canopied bed, taking turns getting up to bathe her forehead with cold compresses. In the morning, assured that there was nothing he could do at home, Proctor finally left the house for the office around 7:30 a.m., an hour later than usual. On the way, one of his carriage horses pulled up lame. He finally arrived at the office just before 10:00. It was now shortly after 2:00 p.m., and Proctor, irritable at the lack of news from the house, was preparing to leave for home when one of the young clerks stuck his head in the door to his office.

"The doctor just sent word that Fannie's out of the woods. The fever broke just before noon. She's sleeping now."

"Thank God." Proctor sat down heavily, relief etched on his face. He suddenly turned impatient. "Why didn't he send word sooner?"

He inhaled deeply and slowly let his breath out. His face was tired and lined.

"She's a terribly weak child," he mused, almost to himself. "Every illness seems to be worse than the last. I'm afraid we are going to lose her yet."

*

Proctor was right. Fannie died in 1883 at the age of nineteen. After the committal service, Emily sent Frank to look for Proctor.

"I'm worried about him," Emily told Frank. "It's been a terrible blow for him. Fannie was always so special to him."

The family and a small number of close friends had returned to Proctor's house after the service. Frank had seen Proctor briefly, greeting people somberly. He looked drawn.

Frank found Proctor sitting on a cemetery marker near Fannie's freshly filled-in gravesite. Here, away from the trees and buildings of the town, the full expanse of the sky stretched over them. Thousands of stars dotted every inch of the vast canopy.

Frank stood uncertainly, not wanting to interrupt or disturb him. *What can I possibly say to the man?* Frank wondered.

"She was so gentle," Proctor mused quietly, not looking at Frank. "She was dealt a raw deal, but she never complained. She had beautiful eyes. Remember her eyes, Frank? How blue they were?" Proctor turned to look at Frank and back at Fannie's grave.

Frank nodded dumbly,

"I took her hand and she opened her eyes and smiled so sweetly at me," Proctor went on quietly. Then she just…left…" Proctor's voice trailed off.

"And smile away my mortal to divine," Frank said softly.

"What was that?" Proctor turned to Frank. "What did you say?"

"It's the last line from a poem by Elizabeth Barrett Browning," Frank replied, suddenly self-conscious.

"What's the rest of it?"

"I don't know it all. Just the ending." Frank said, embarrassed.

"Yes? Tell me."

"Oh Christ, come tenderly," Frank began softly, almost prayerfully. "And stoop thyself to gather my life's rose. And smile away my mortal to divine."

Neither of the men said anything. Frank felt awkward and embarrassed after his recitation. *Why did I let my emotions take control of me?* he wondered. *What would Proctor think?*

"And smile away my mortal to divine," Proctor repeated slowly. "Christ come tenderly. And stoop to gather my life's rose."

His voice was halting and thick with emotion. "And smile away my mortal to divine."

"Mrs. Browning was an invalid most of her young life," Frank told him. "But she has written some of the most beautiful words I have ever read."

"Gather my life's rose, and smile away my mortal to divine," Proctor repeated again. He looked at Frank. Tears filled his eyes.

"Thank you," he said hoarsely. "Let's go home. Fannie's all right now."

*

Proctor felt distracted after the clerk told him that Fannie's fever had broken. He might as well go home. This day had been a disaster. He had not accomplished anything.

"There's a Mrs. Myers in the waiting room to see you," the clerk continued after giving Proctor the news about Fannie.

"Mrs. Myers?"

"She says you knew her husband, John Myers."

Proctor pushed back his chair, eager at the diversion and chance to take his mind off Fannie.

"John Myers? Of course I knew John. Wonderful fellow. I was very sorry to hear of his death. I wonder what his widow could want. What was her name?"

"Mary," the clerk said.

"Mary Myers. Yes, of course. Must be some problem with the estate, not that John had much of one. From all accounts, he owed everybody in town. By all means, show her in."

Proctor had known John Myers casually as a solid, if overly cautious, businessman unfortunately drawn into partnership with Dorr. He had never met his wife, Mary.

She entered his office quietly, a slim, graceful woman. She was still dressed in mourning clothes, black dress and hat. Short, wavy, soft brown curls cascaded from under her hat and framed a delicate face. She was short, even dainty looking despite the heavy dress that was gathered tightly at her waist, exaggerating her breasts and hips in the style of the day. Her clothes were expensive but well worn, he noticed. Proctor knew from local gossip that the marble mill was very nearly bankrupt, and that her husband's sudden death had made her destitute. But he never would have known it by looking at this self-possessed creature in front of him. He rose to greet her.

"How do you do, Mr. Proctor," she said, extending him a gloved hand. "Thank you for seeing me."

"The pleasure is all mine. John was a dear friend. I was very saddened to learn of his passing."

He took her arm lightly and steered her to a small humpback sofa in front of the fireplace. He sat opposite her in a tall straight-backed, tapestry-upholstered chair.

"May I offer you some refreshment?" he asked.

"No. Please, I'm fine."

She took off her hat and set it next to her on the sofa, shaking her hair to loosen it. It fell thick and wavy, without a trace of gray, down her back and around her shoulders.

Proctor smiled at her. "How is it that we have never met?"

"John was not well. We seldom went places because of his health."

Proctor knew that the Myerses seldom went places because everywhere they might have gone, they would have run into people to whom they owed money.

"I liked John very much," Proctor said. "I wish I had seen him more often."

"You are very kind, Mr. Proctor."

Proctor's breath quickened as she smiled at him. How very calm and composed she is, he observed. Not at all like Emily.

"Please stop all this 'Mr. Proctor' nonsense," he told her. "I insist you call me Redfield."

"Very well—Redfield," she hesitated just slightly as she said his name. "And you must call me Mary."

"Well," he said with satisfaction. "Now that we have introduced ourselves, how might I be of service to you?"

"You are very kind."

Proctor nodded.

"My husband spoke very highly of you."

Proctor said nothing. Her voice was so soft he had to strain to hear her.

"Redfield," she said, smiling at him, "as you know, my husband was in partnership with Seneca Dorr in the marble mill at Sutherland Falls. It was a disastrous partnership. John was much too easy-going to be in business. His heart was not in it. I loved him for his compassion. He was the gentlest, kindest man I have ever known. But the same qualities I loved in him made him a terrible businessman. He was not hard enough to be in business. People often took advantage of his generosity."

Proctor nodded. He knew John Myers had extended credit to many people who had never paid him and never had any intention of paying him.

"And Seneca," Mary's voice hardened, "Seneca took advantage of John more than anyone. John might have been a poor businessman, but Seneca was completely irresponsible. He argued constantly with John. Any decision John made, Seneca took the opposite view just to be contrary. He knew nothing about how marble should be milled, nothing about prices. He promised customers impossible delivery dates. He knew nothing about scheduling. Machinery would break and stand idle for weeks for want of a simple part. And anything John tried to do, Seneca fought him on it. The accounts are in shambles because of him. I blame Seneca for the mill's failure and for John's death."

"What can I do? How can I help?" Proctor asked.

"You can help me stop Seneca from selling the mill."

"Seneca wants to sell the mill?"

"Yes." She laughed bitterly. "Sell is hardly the word. He has no concept of what the mill is worth."

As she sat in his office, destitute, Proctor knew, by her husband's sudden death, Mary did not betray a hint of her financial plight in her face or voice. Proctor was impressed.

"What do you think should be done?" he asked her.

Proctor had never met a woman whom he felt comfortable discussing business with, but with Mary, it seemed the most natural thing in the world to do.

"Milling is only half the marble business," Mary replied. "By itself, milling will never be profitable. Even with the cheap waterpower we get from the falls, the company, as it is, has only very limited potential. But if we could consolidate the milling operation at Sutherland Falls with the marble quarries in the area, we would have control of the whole process. The quarries in this area are among the largest in the world. We haven't even begun to come to the end of some of them. There are quarries that haven't even been unearthed yet. The supply of marble is limitless and the quality is some of the highest in the world. If we could bring all the operations together, in one company, we could dominate the business."

"Hmmm. That's an interesting idea," Proctor mused.

The only thing Proctor knew about marble was that it came out of the ground and that it took prodigious numbers of men and beasts to work it. As far as he knew, none of the many small quarries and mills around Rutland County did much more than scratch out a living, if indeed they made any money at all.

"I understand the quarries here are of exceptionally fine quality, and the deposits are quite extensive," he said. "But none of them has ever made any money. How can they be made profitable?"

"Those new quarries near Danby that have just been uncovered are estimated to extend all the way back under Danby Mountain," Mary told him. "The stone is some of the finest imperial marble in the world."

"Imperial?" Proctor asked. "I'm not familiar with that type."

"It's an extremely pure white marble. Very hard and dense. Excellent for monumental and decorative work," Mary said. "You can practically see yourself in it when it is polished. In West Rutland, the deposits are more cream colored. The marble is very hard and translucent and can be veined or mottled and clouded with gray or green. It polishes beautifully. Not counting the various grades of blue marble, the West Rutland vein produces fifteen different grades of marble, ranging from almost pure white to dark greens. Most of that marble is mainly used for building and monument work. And right here at Sutherland Falls, the marble is more bluish gray. Very high quality. Excellent for building. Vermont probably contains the greatest variety of marble anywhere in the world."

"Really?" Proctor asked, impressed. "I had no idea."

"There are nearly one hundred different commercial varieties in the state," she told him.

"Besides tombstones and buildings, what are some of the other uses of marble?" Proctor asked.

"Tombstones!" Mary exclaimed. She leaned back in her chair, her breasts heaving with laughter.

"What's wrong?" he protested. "What did I say?"

"The first thing you must learn, Mr. Proctor, is never to say, 'tombstones!'" Mary sat up, still laughing. "The proper term is 'monument' work."

"All right, all right," he groused, feigning offense. "I stand corrected in the lady's presence. Besides a few cemetery markers…"

"Excuse me?" Mary asked, looking coyly up at him.

"I mean monuments," he conceded. "Who besides a few corpses are interested in buying marble?"

Mary laughed again. "Don't knock the corpse market," she told him. "Eventually, we all become part of it."

"Later, rather than sooner, I hope," Proctor replied.

They both laughed. Proctor had forgotten his earlier irritation and worry and fatigue. Mary's face was flushed with color.

"Seriously," she said, composing herself. "There are three major commercial uses of marble in this country: monument work, structural uses in buildings and decorative work."

"Vermont marble is used for all three?"

"Oh my, yes."

"But no new or existing quarry that has opened around here has ever made a go of it. As far as I know, they have all been losing propositions. How can it be made profitable?" he asked her again. "I have heard that some of those quarries are over eight hundred feet deep. It must cost a fortune to get those blocks to the mill."

"Yes," she conceded. "Transportation is the key ingredient in the marble business. Right now, the blocks are mostly hauled to the mill in horse-drawn carts or with oxen. It's a very slow and tedious and costly process. But," she leaned forward in her chair, "the mill is located right on the railroad line. If we were to construct short extensions off the rail line right onto the quarry floor, we'd save enormously on our transportation costs."

From the beginning, Mary Myers had talked like they were already partners: We, ours, us. Proctor had not even noticed, so subtle and natural was their relationship.

She continued: "We've already got the most important transport link—hauling the sawed blocks to market—in place, thanks to the rail line that runs right next to the falls. If we were to extend short trunks off that line right onto the quarry floors, we'd solve the other major transport problem—getting the rough stones from the quarry to the mill."

"Yes." Proctor was thoughtful. "The rail line would be a very big savings."

He stroked his beard. "But you still need hundreds of men to work those quarries—there's no getting around that. My God, the labor costs would be exorbitant. Everything must be done by hand."

"Labor is the cheapest part of the process," Mary replied. "Every day thousands of immigrants arrive in New York Harbor. Many of them worked the stone quarries in their native countries. They are already trained and used to hard work. And they're cheaper to house and feed than cattle, and more productive."

Proctor smiled at her. Mary, leaning forward, smiled back, drawing him into her confidence. "And I have just seen a demonstration of a new way of extracting marble that will make quarrying even cheaper and faster and less wasteful," she said. "It's quite transformed the business in Europe already."

"What is that?" Proctor asked.

"It's called a wire saw."

"I've never heard of it."

"It was patented about fifteen years ago, 1854 to be exact."

"I must have missed it."

She laughed. "That's too bad, because it may very well transform your life."

Now it was his turn to laugh.

"Please don't keep me in suspense," he said. "How does it work?"

"Wires are twisted 'round each other and attached to pulleys at either end. Two men pull the wires back and forth across the marble, using sand as an abrasive and water to cool it. The friction of the wires moving back and forth can cut the marble faster than a dozen men using chisels and sledgehammers. It's going to revolutionize the way marble is quarried."

They talked on and on. Proctor had not felt so energized since the war.

"It would be foolish to sell the mill as Dorr wants," Mary told him. "It's the centerpiece of the whole operation. We already have the falls for power and the rail line for shipping. We've got the mill for cutting and polishing. All we need is the marble. If we could consolidate the quarries in the area and bring them into the operation, we'd have a monopoly on the business."

"Yes, yes." Proctor finally said, stroking his beard and glancing sideways at her. "I think we can prevent Dorr from selling the mill."

He saw her visibly relax. Her clear blue eyes met his in a glow of warmth and secret confidences.

From the beginning, Mary Myers and Proctor communicated on a different level. They discussed everything. At first, the bond that drew them together was their mutual distaste for Dorr. Later, it was a common thirst for power and money. They were mirror images of each other, their thoughts jumping across the room to one another almost before their words. Although Proctor knew next to nothing about marble, he did know about law and about people. He listened carefully to Mary, who did know about marble and also about people.

Their first action was to get Proctor appointed receiver of the mill, an easy matter for Proctor, who knew the judge in the bankruptcy hearing. Next, they bought out Dorr. Dorr protested loudly and bitterly over the price, but with Proctor wielding unlimited control over the finances of the company, Dorr could do nothing other than accept the offer. Proctor, with Mary close, but discreetly, by his side, then turned his attention to the mill's accounts, straightening them out with such success that, within a few weeks of his takeover, the company turned its first profit.

In November 1870, exactly one year after he first entered the marble trade, Proctor acquired the Massachusetts-owned Sutherland Falls Marble Company, which owned the quarries near the falls. The new Vermont

Marble quarry at Proctor, Vermont, showing workers at the bottom. *From the collection of the University of California at Riverside, California Museum of Photography.*

corporation Proctor organized was also called the Sutherland Falls Marble Company, and it listed Proctor as treasurer and resident manager. As Mary Myers had predicted when she first enlisted Proctor's help, the new company reaped enormous benefits by consolidating the operations of the two nearby properties. For the first time in the region, all the quarrying, milling and shipping operations of the newly flourishing marble trade were under the control of one company—and one man. Within ten years, the business had doubled and doubled and doubled again, and Sutherland Falls marble was known all over the world.

Redfield Proctor would not have to practice law after all.

Chapter 5

LIBRARY

Seneca was in fine form this afternoon," Frank observed.

Frank, Redfield and Fletcher Proctor were in Proctor's big house by the falls. Supper was over, and they had retired as usual to Redfield's private, comfortably furnished study off the library for a cigar. This room was Proctor's favorite. It was smaller and more intimate than either the library or his office in Center Rutland, where he conducted most of his public business. This room was the private man: light, cozy, decorated simply. A large framed oil painting of Traveler, Proctor's Civil War mount, hung over the fireplace. Traveler had died some years before after siring numerous descendants and was buried near the house under a slab of white marble. Proctor's favorite hunting gun hung on another wall. All around were hunting mementos and pictures from the war, from politics and from hunting and fishing expeditions. The closest thing to a family portrait was a picture of Proctor with his three favorite tracking dogs on the far wall.

Fletcher Proctor, who was the same age as Frank Partridge, twenty-six, but looked at least ten years older, got up, sauntered over to the brandy decanter and poured himself a large glass. He shuffled back across the room and threw himself into his chair by the fireplace. He was taller than his father, not fat, but with a slight paunch and a fleshy, unhealthy pallor to his face. While his father was ramrod straight, Fletcher slouched when he stood. His clothes were expensive but ill-fitting. His handkerchief was usually soiled, his boots scuffed and dirty. Already, he was going bald.

"Ahh, he's always been jealous because we succeeded here where he ought to have," Fletcher said. The 'we' was as expansive as the drink he washed it down with.

Redfield looked disapprovingly at his son's glass. He had strong prohibitionist views and rarely took a drink himself. The brandy decanter was kept for mostly medicinal purposes. Noticing his father's gaze, Fletcher tossed back his head and drained the contents, setting the glass down hard on the table next to him.

"You know how I feel about drinking in the house," Proctor said quietly.

"Would you rather I went down to the tavern?"

It was a faceoff Frank had seen repeated numerous times. The father and son stared at one another, neither giving in. Almost out of habit, Frank glanced discreetly at his timepiece, subconsciously timing the showdown he knew would end the way it usually did.

"You're right about Dorr," Proctor finally said, glancing away from his son.

As Frank knew would happen, it was Redfield who acquiesced. Frank shifted slightly in his chair to get a better view of Redfield. No emotion showed on the father's face. Redfield turned abruptly away from his son and stared into the fire, slowly crossing his fingers. Fletcher shot a glance of triumph in Frank's direction. Frank ignored him.

"Those ragged Democrats," Redfield went on, shaking his head disdainfully. "They are so self-righteous. Dorr married into money. His own family had money. He's never had to work a day in his life. Yet, he thinks he knows what is best for a bunch of sweaty, ignorant laborers who wouldn't have a dime for a loaf of bread if I had not given them a job. Half of these immigrants can't even speak English. The other half are illiterate. They don't care what party represents them in the legislature. They don't even know what a legislature is."

Proctor turned toward Frank and Fletcher.

"The general impression is that the labor element will make a strong effort to carry the spring elections and try to get hold of the machinery of town government-listers, overseer of the poor, selectmen. We mustn't let the Democrats in here to organize the workers. They've already succeeded in electing the first-ever Democratic representative from Rutland in history to the state legislature. If we do not act now, they will continue to make inroads. Common sense tells us the labor element outnumber us. Our only chance of turning back the rising labor tide is to divide them. In a large town, the votes of the working men are anonymous. But if we can divide Rutland into smaller towns, we can regain control of their votes. What sandblaster in Proctor would not vote Republican if I told him to? What quarryman in West Rutland would vote Democratic if I told him to vote Republican? No stone crusher would dare go against my wishes—at least not if he wanted to keep his job. But in a large town like Rutland, all of them can vote any way they please with impunity. No, our only hope of keeping our Republican majority is to divide the town into smaller towns where we can control the votes of the workers in Proctor and West Rutland. We already know Rutland Center can be counted on to vote Republican. It's the labor element we have to get control of. But you know what provokes me most in this whole struggle?" Proctor asked. "Just where would labor be without jobs? When was the last time Dorr and the Democrats created jobs the way the Republicans have? The way I have? Dorr had his chance here and failed. Now he makes a name for himself attacking me because I succeeded where he did not."

"Especially with Mary Myers," Fletcher broke in lazily. "Just think what Dorr would say if he knew about *that*. What a field day the Democrats would have if they knew that the strait-laced Republican ex-governor who passed the strictest divorce law in state history was having an extramarital affair! Whoo-eee! Talk about sparks!" Fletcher chuckled loudly.

It was moments like these that Frank wondered most at Proctor's tolerance. The father and son were so different. There had always been talk—mostly crude barroom innuendos or polite drawing room gossip—about how different the two were.

"It's really hard to believe sometimes that they are father and son," women would cluck disapprovingly to their neighbors after one of Fletcher's latest escapades.

"Well, you know, Redfield was off at the war when Fletcher was born."

"Oh hush. That was Fannie who was born while Redfield was away fighting."

"You don't suppose Fannie is…?"

"Now stop spreading rumors! Emily Dutton is one of the finest women I know. And what she has to put up with from that Fletcher! And poor Fannie. So sickly all the time and such a sweet girl. It's just a shame how things turn out."

Frank still remembered the first time he had met Fletcher. He remembered staring at a pale, skinny fourteen-year-old boy and trying to recall something he had once heard about him. The boy looked harmless, even scared, but Frank could not shake that lingering doubt.

It was late fall of 1874 when Frank first met Proctor and Fletcher. School had started more than two months earlier. At that time, it was customary for high school–age boys to 'board out.' So even though the Partridges lived in East Middlebury, Frank took a room during the school term with Mrs. Potter, a middle-aged widow who lived in Middlebury. In exchange for light chores around the house, Frank received his room and two meals a day.

"Fraaaaaank. Oh, Fraaaaaaank," Mrs. Potter called to him as she slowly made her way up the stairs, wheezing heavily. Mrs. Potter had a bad heart and did not often climb the stairs to his room in the attic, so Frank knew something must be up for her to come all the way up to get him.

"Frank," Mrs. Potter whispered between gasps for air. She was standing outside his door. "A young man from Rutland and his father are downstairs. The boy has just enrolled at Middlebury and is looking for a place to board here in town."

"What's his name?" Frank opened the door a crack and looked out at Mrs. Potter. She was sweating slightly and still breathing heavily from her slow climb up the stairs.

"Proctor," Mrs. Potter said. She leaned toward Frank and spoke in a hushed, confidential tone. "Mattie Squires says Mr. Proctor is the richest man in Rutland. He certainly looks it, too, the way he's all dressed up so nice in a suit and all. Mattie says the boy, now what was his name? It wasn't Frank, but something like that. Well, anyway, Mattie says the boy is a real hell-raiser."

Mrs. Potter kept looking over her shoulder back down the stairs. She wet her lips and continued in a low voice.

"It's hard to believe. He's so pale and kind of weak looking. But Mattie says he's caused his father all kinds of trouble. Now, normally," she smoothed her apron with her hands, "I don't like noisy or troublesome boys, you know that. But Mr. Proctor is so important and all, that I'm willing to make an exception this one time."

"What kind of trouble?" Frank liked having the room to himself.

"Well now, I don't know, but his father is very anxious to meet you and to have his son room with you."

"Why me?" Frank asked, reluctantly opening the door. "I've never heard of him before."

"Well, I'm sure I don't know, Frank," Mrs. Potter hissed quietly, exasperation creeping into her voice. "It's the middle of the term, and there aren't many rooms left in town for the boys. I'm surprised they even let him enroll in the middle like this. Mr. Proctor has inquired around town and says this is the only room he could find for his son—darned if I can remember his name. Now go downstairs, Frank. They're waiting for you. And please be polite."

A roommate was the last thing Frank wanted. He liked his privacy. He was a quiet, studious boy, almost taciturn. He had few close friends at school and liked it that way. He did not like loud noises or loud people. Reluctantly, he went downstairs.

The man he met downstairs in the small front parlor was the most important-looking man Frank had ever seen. At fourteen, Frank was easily impressed by wealth and power, and he had never seen so much of either in one man before. He shook hands firmly with Proctor, sizing up his expensive clothes and manicured nails and appearance with an appreciative eye. Finally, he turned to look at the boy by Proctor's side, measuring him in the same steady reserved manner, as Fletcher fidgeted and looked bored. Proctor watched Frank's every move. Years later, Proctor told Frank it was the young boy's cool maturity at that meeting that had first caught his fancy.

"Right from the beginning, I saw something special in you," Proctor told Frank. "Of course, it never hurt that you said a kind word about my favorite horse tethered outside," he added with a large chuckle. "You know Frank, the best way to judge a man is by the horse he rides."

And so the bond had been struck. For a long time, Frank had not cared very much for Fletcher. Even now, he did not really like him, although he found himself irresistibly attracted by him and could not help admiring—was it admiration or envy?—Fletcher's total self-possession and the hold he exercised over his father. In a family dynasty, the genes often die quickly. In Proctor's case, there was little before him and not much more after him, although his two sons and a grandson continued to bask in his bright glow despite their own low wattage long after Proctor's death.

It was a continual source of amazement to Frank, this mammoth flaw called Fletcher in Redfield's character. With his other children, Proctor was demanding and relentless in the extreme, although he obviously loved his children dearly. That love, however, did not stop him from demanding much of his children. But with his first-born son, Proctor was uncharacteristically soft. Proctor's own childhood had been unhappy. His father died when he was eight, and Proctor had to shoulder the responsibilities of the family at an early age. He seemed somehow determined that his own eldest son should know none of the hardships and unhappiness of Proctor's own childhood.

"Boys will be boys," Proctor would often remark after one of Fletcher's lapses. "He's just having a little harmless fun."

Proctor never seemed to grasp the fact that pandering to a weak character such as his son's was like a life sentence to immaturity.

Fletcher's first lapse after meeting Frank happened only a few years later when Fletcher was caught cheating on his exams at Middlebury College. For the first time, Frank became aware of his own place in the odd father/son relationship that existed between Proctor and Fletcher. Frank had never seen Proctor angry with Fletcher before, and like every strong emotion between the father and son, it was quickly deflected onto Frank.

"Why did you cheat on the examination?" Proctor asked Fletcher sternly.

"Because if I didn't, I would have failed," Fletcher told his father, looking surprised at the question.

"And just how do you propose to pass when you are kicked out of the school for cheating?"

"I'm sorry Father, but it's nothing none of the other boys don't do—everyone except Frank, of course. I just happened to be the unlucky one who got caught, that's all. All the boys do it. I'm sure if you were to speak to the president, he would take me back."

After Fletcher had left the room, Proctor turned on Frank.

"I'm very disappointed in you, Frank. Especially after everything we have done for you."

"But why, sir?" Frank blurted, stunned at Proctor's accusation.

"I don't like the idea that my son should be caught cheating. Think of his poor mother, and the shame it should bring to the family."

"But what was I supposed to do about it?"

"He's your roommate, isn't he? Don't you come down here on your holidays from school to work in the office? Didn't I lend you the money for college? Aren't you Fletcher's constant companion? Isn't he your best friend?"

Frank had never really considered himself and Fletcher friends. It was Proctor that Frank liked being around. Fletcher was just something they both had in common. And Frank really thought Proctor was fond of him, too, that it was Proctor who liked having him around, that it was Proctor who wanted Frank to come down and work in the office on school holidays and vacations, almost—Frank hardly dared think the thought—like his son, his real son, not this rogue of a son. Frank suddenly felt very confused by this man he adored.

"Yes sir," Frank answered Proctor, his voice flat, his face blank, betraying none of the emotions he was feeling.

"Frank," Proctor's voice suddenly softened, and he came from around his desk to put his hand on the boy's shoulder. Any other time, Frank would have cherished the gesture for weeks. Today, he stood as stony and unfeeling as a cold hard slab of marble.

"Frank, Fletcher is not like you. He's wild and full of oats. He doesn't like to study. Bookwork comes hard to him. He likes to be out with the boys, raising Cain and having fun. But he's a good boy, and a smart boy, too. He may not have a lot of book sense like you, but he has a good head on his shoulders. The two of you have a bright future ahead of you. You complement each other like a pair of well-matched horses. One headstrong, one calm and sensible. Fletcher is wild and enthusiastic. You are thoughtful and reserved. The two of you make a good team. One day, the two of you will take over this company. But Frank, you must not ever forget that Fletcher is a Proctor. Proctors have certain responsibilities. Proctors have a responsibility to this community. They have to be protected from harm and from people who might want to hurt them or embarrass them in some way. And Lord knows, Fletcher needs protecting, especially from himself. Think of his poor mother and what this whole cheating scandal would do to her if she ever finds out. People expect a higher standard from Proctors. I know it's not fair, but they do anyway. We have been given much and, as a result, much is expected of us and of the people around us. Do you understand that, Frank?"

Frank nodded.

"Fletcher would do anything to help you and to protect you. You know that don't you, Frank?"

Frank wasn't so sure, but he nodded again anyway.

"And I expect the same sort of loyalty from you on Fletcher's behalf. Is that clear, Frank?"

And that was how Fletcher came to pass the Latin test that was required for admission into Amherst College without ever showing up for the exam. Fletcher was wrong. A few words from his father were not enough to get him reinstated at Middlebury, thanks to a God-fearing president who believed he was put on this earth to make life miserable for the rich and powerful. Fletcher was out for good at Middlebury, and in Proctor's strict litmus test of loyalty, that meant Frank was out for good, too. But unlike Fletcher, Frank learned his lessons well. He had always been a quick study, and he knew now what was expected of him. When Fletcher, who was as weak in the classics, as he was in most things scholastic, needed to pass a Latin test to gain admission into Amherst, Frank did not have to be asked. He volunteered to take the exam for him.

And so Fletcher got into Amherst, graduating with Frank in 1882. With his school days mercifully over, Fletcher started his career at the marble company. Proctor was not worried about his son's future. He knew Frank, who went on to graduate from Columbia University Law School in 1884, before also returning to work in the company, would be smart enough for both of the boys.

Chapter 6

OFFICE

Frank stood in front of the looking glass on the wall in his outer office and cleared his throat. He gazed at his reflection, smiled self-consciously and quickly turned serious again. He was a handsome young man with large, prominent eyes and thick, bushy brows. A year ago, imitating his mentor, Proctor, he had grown a beard, which he kept neatly trimmed. He moistened his lips and glanced down at the paper he held in his left hand. He looked up again, caught his eye in the glass, straightened his shoulders and began reading.

"My love for you is like a river,

"Clear, deep, wide and endless…"

"Good morning, Frank," Proctor opened the door to the office and strode into the room. A rush of air entered with him.

"Sir! What are you doing here so early?"

Frank crumbled the paper in his hand and pretended to straighten his collar in the glass. He gave it a little yank and turned red faced toward Proctor. He arched his neck and tried to look down at his shirt front, still pretending to be absorbed in his collar.

"I wasn't expecting you so early," Frank said, finally looking up at Proctor. Proctor smiled at his discomfort.

"Are you reading tonight?" he asked.

"Uhh, reading?" Frank crammed the crumpled poem into his breast pocket. "Reading? Uh, why, uh, yes, as a matter of fact, I am," he finally stammered. "Julia has invited Miss Louisa May Alcott from Boston to tonight's meeting of the Fortnightly Society. I'm reading one of my poems."

"Excellent," Proctor replied, genuinely impressed. "Louisa May Alcott! Even I have heard of her. I'm sure you will do fine. I have never been much of one for poetry, myself, but I understand Julia is exceptionally talented at it."

"Oh, she really is, sir!" Frank enthused. "She has had a number of her poems published by some of the leading magazines. She is very highly regarded. She used to correspond regularly with Ralph Waldo Emerson before he died, and Henry Thoreau, too."

"You don't say," Proctor said. "I must admit that I have never heard of Thoreau, but everyone knows Mr. Emerson and, of course, Miss Alcott. I take it she's a friend of Julia's?"

"Yes, yes, she is. A *very* good friend," Frank replied.

"How can someone as talented and respected as Julia Caroline Ripley, from one of the best and most prominent families in New England, marry a gadfly like Dorr? It's a strange combination, at best."

"It is hard to understand," Frank agreed, pulling at his collar again. The conversation was entering dangerous ground: guilt by association. *Why was I so clumsy?* Frank wondered. He was afraid Proctor's good humor and the respect he held for Julia Dorr might vanish at the mention of her husband, Seneca Dorr, clouding not only Proctor's warm feelings toward Julia but perhaps even spreading to Julia's acquaintances—like himself.

The Fortnightly Society, which Julia Caroline Ripley Dorr had started, was one of Frank's passions. The group of young men and women from Rutland met every two weeks to act out small scenes from Shakespeare, discuss literary topics and read from their own works. Frank was one of the group's most loyal members and often presided at meetings when Julia was away at one of her own readings out of state or attending another literary function. Frank did not want Proctor to disapprove of his membership in the group just because Julia happened to be married to Dorr.

He groped to change the subject. Too late. He saw the beginnings of a frown spreading over Proctor's face.

"Is it true that Julia has been tutoring some of the laborers on their English?" Proctor asked, his tone all at once businesslike and direct. "I heard that and was quite dismayed. I don't think it is a good thing if she is. The less English these men learn the better."

"I know that she helps anyone who comes to her," Frank responded vaguely. "She is very generous with her time and her talents."

"It's one thing to encourage the young men and women of the town to develop their literary interests and talents," Proctor said. "It's quite another to be teaching the working men."

Frank tried to change the conversation. "I have heard she teaches an English class, but I had no idea that it was for the workers. I can find out if you like."

He hoped that would end the subject.

"Please do," Proctor said. "It would be a dangerous thing for the men to get too proficient in English. Look at the trouble we've had with that fellow Sundqvist. Why, just yesterday I had to send a whole shipment of Italians right back to John Allen, our Boston agent. They could speak English as well as anybody. They even said Allen promised them eleven dollars a month. Imagine that! I told Allen from now on to send us only stout, green men fresh from the old soil. I don't want any who have been in America awhile, and I certainly don't want any to misunderstand their pay. The less English they know, the better."

"I'll get off a note this morning to all of the agents," Frank replied, thankful the conversation was back on a business footing.

He moved over to his desk and picked up a paper. "Before I forget, Henry Hall, a Rutland historian, has asked me to request the favor of a portrait of yourself for a history he is writing of the county."

"Henry Hall? Isn't he a member of the Fortnightly Society?"

Frank blushed, cursing himself for allowing the conversation to return to the society again after they had apparently left it. He knew Proctor had mentioned the society on purpose just to show Frank he had not forgotten. He was surprised Proctor even knew that Hall was a member. Hall was a Rutland shopkeeper who Proctor knew only slightly. The Fortnightly Society was the least of Hall's accomplishments and certainly not the one Proctor knew him by.

"Yes, as a matter of fact, he is," Frank replied.

"Why does he want a portrait of me? Doesn't he know I am not a native of the county? My residence here has been comparatively brief to be included in any history of the county."

"Of course, you're right, sir. It's really not appropriate. I should have told him so myself and not bothered you."

"Yes, I hardly think my portrait would add anything to a history of Rutland County, unless," Proctor paused, belaboring the conversation, enjoying himself and Frank's discomfort, "unless, of course, his object is to put together a history of men noted for their personal beauty. In that case, I should be happy to oblige him."

Why did I allow myself to fall into this trap!? Frank didn't know if Proctor was giving him the go-ahead to use his portrait or simply making fun of him. He chuckled weakly.

"Yes sir, I'll tell him."

Frank cleared his throat. "On another matter, sir, Arabella desires to join the Daughters of the American Revolution. If you approve, the annual membership fee is one dollar."

Arabella was the oldest of Proctor's five children and a year older than Fletcher and Frank.

"Of course, I approve," Proctor replied. "Both the Proctors and the Duttons on her mother's side have many relatives who fought in that war. She could be a member on either side, although I'd be happy to certify to the Daughters that 'Bella should be entitled in her own right to join any warlike association."

Frank smiled and didn't say anything. He was very fond of 'Bella, who had her father's quick wit, flashing eyes and passion for political debate. Frank often wished 'Bella had been the first-born son instead of Fletcher.

"I notified Fletcher you wanted to meet with the two of us at nine o'clock this morning," he said.

"Good. We've got a lot of work to do." Proctor opened the door to his office that led off from Frank's. A fire was burning in the fireplace and a stack of papers was already piled high on top of his huge, but otherwise neat, wooden desk.

"I put this morning's papers on your desk, sir," Frank said. "The testimony before the legislative committee yesterday afternoon was quite heated. It appears that Dorr was just the warmup. It got very hot. I compiled a summary of it from this morning's *Herald* and typed it up for you."

"Thank you." Proctor sat down behind his desk. "It looks like I am going to have to go to Washington next Wednesday and Thursday after all to figure the new job for the grand entrance to the west front of the Capitol. It's poor timing, what with the committee hearings and all, but there's no way around it. I have put them off for as long as I dare. Would you make the arrangements?"

"Of course. Will Mrs. Myers be traveling with you?"

"Ahh, that's another problem," Proctor sighed. "Emily's decided to go with me. She says she's worried lately about my going about alone so much."

"I'm sure she is simply worried about your health, sir," Frank said diplomatically. "I'm sure that's all it means."

"Yes, yes. Try telling that to Mary."

Proctor picked up several sheets from the stack on his desk, glanced at them and looked up at Frank. "All of this is from yesterday's hearing?"

"Yes sir. It lasted well into the evening."

"Was any of it favorable?" Proctor asked thumbing through the pages.

"Only William Page, the manager of Howe Scale Works in Rutland."

"Page? What'd he say?"

"He said he didn't see any way Rutland would be hurt by division."

Proctor laughed. "That's it? That was the extent of our support?"

"Pretty much. Page told the committee that was his own personal opinion of the matter, and that he was not influenced by you or under any personal obligation to you."

"The hell he isn't," Proctor snorted. "Anything else?"

"When Page said he was under no obligation to you, somebody asked him if you weren't his bondsman."

"What'd he say?"

"He said, 'Governor Proctor is not my bondsman as manager of Howe Scale Works.' So then somebody asked him if you were his personal bondsman."

"And?"

"He said, 'Governor Proctor is not my personal bondsman, although he is the bondsman of the administrator of my father's estate.'"

Proctor laughed heartily. "Good old Page. Did anybody ask him who the administrator of his father's estate is?"

"No," Frank replied.

"Page is!" Proctor chuckled. "He is the administrator of his father's estate! Ha, ha, ha. Good old Page. Draft him a letter this morning, will you? Tell him how much I enjoyed his testimony. Ha, ha, ha," Proctor laughed again. "With support like that I can't wait to see the opposition."

He picked up the stack and began scanning it quickly. A frown slowly spread over his face as he read.

"You say everything here is opposed?" He looked up at Frank.

"Yes, and that's not even all of it," Frank said. "It went on for several hours. The paper said nearly every man in the hall spoke."

Proctor put the stack back down on his desk, thinking hard, his good humor evaporated.

"Damn that Dorr," he muttered quietly. "I blame him for this. Just because he made a mess of this business..." His voice trailed off. He looked up at Frank.

"You know I don't mind the fact that there's opposition to us or that people are speaking up against us. In fact, I'd be disappointed if there wasn't some opposition. I don't even mind the personal attacks. But this business Dorr is putting out about the 'foreign corporation' and the 'New York corporation' trying to buy a seat in our legislature. That galls me no end. I control this company, not the New York interest. Yet, they make it sound as if I were some kind of puppet for the New York interest, some kind of carpetbagger exploiting the state of Vermont and taking all of the profit, and even a seat in the legislature, back to New York! I can't abide that. No one loves this state more than I do. It is true, we will get two extra legislative seats out of this division, but you can be sure they will not go to the New York interest! *I* control this company. *I* control this town. Not the New York interest."

Proctor's face was set in determination.

"I know one thing," he continued, his voice low and measured. "As soon as this fight is over, Smedburg is out. If it's the last thing I do, I will break his power. New York corporation! Ha! We'll see about that."

He looked hard at Frank. "Once this township flap has quieted down, I'm dropping the directors who act with Smedburg, and then I'm dropping Smedburg. I am not going to transmit the burden of contending with that man on to you boys."

Chapter 7

QUARRY

"The boys," as Proctor called them, were both still at Amherst the first time Frank met the infamous Adolphus Smedburg.

It was the summer of 1879, and Frank was down for the summer working and learning the business as he had done since first meeting Proctor and Fletcher five years before.

It was a brilliant, late June day—spectacular. A hot sun beat down on Frank from a cloudless, deep blue sky. Its warmth felt good on his face after the long winter months of classrooms and schoolwork, and he inhaled deeply the dizzying perfume of the forests and grassy meadows as he rode to the West Rutland quarry.

By now, Frank was used to the noise and confusion that greeted him on the quarry floor. In fact, he now knew that it wasn't confusion at all but a highly orchestrated and well-oiled assembly line of activity. Every man, beast and machine had a purpose. As he looked around, he nodded to himself at the familiar shouts and roar of machinery. He knew every line of this play, its familiarity almost pleasant. Through the whine of wire saws and explosions of black powder, men—like ants—crawled everywhere. Frank's gaze focused on a group of eight or nine quarrymen slowly lowering themselves on ropes over the top of the quarry wall across from him. They descended about halfway down the quarry face, some two hundred feet above Frank. They had sledgehammers slung over their backs and smaller chisels and crowbars tucked in belts around their waists. They fanned out across a block of rough blue marble like a group of tiny insects, their naked torsos already blackened by the sun. Bracing their feet against the quarry face, the rope slings taut around their chests and under their buttocks, they hammered a line of iron gibs along the top and two sides of the chalked off block. Above the general din, Frank could hear the *Whack! Whack!* as they swung their great hammers high over their heads. Sweat gleamed on their bare backs, arms bulged. Around the quarry that was at least two hundred yards wide, another dozen or so similar crews worked to extract the great blocks of marble. Some of them used hammers, like the crew above him; others pulled screaming wire saws across the blocks. After pounding a line of wedges into the marble, the crew above Frank grunted and sweated as they slowly pried the block loose with levers and crowbars. With one final grunt and push, the twenty-five- by twenty-five-foot block broke cleanly from its base, turning slowly over onto a bed of branches and crushed rock other men had prepared. The stone slid in a cloud of dust down the steep quarry face twenty feet to the top of one of the uppermost terraces of the quarry.

The quarry was an old one, and by now, its face was several hundred feet above the floor where Frank stood, slightly sweating in the blinding sun. Not counting all of the various grades of blue marble, the vein produced fifteen different types of marble for monument and building purposes, ranging from almost pure white to dark green. This particular block was a blue one and looked to be of exceptionally high quality, Frank judged. He looked at his notepad.

"Some of our orders for common blue are being filled with too good stock," he read in Proctor's handwriting. "We don't want to ship anything too good when a poorer grade would do just as well."

Frank squinted up at the block where it had come to rest on the narrow, sloped terrace. Already several quarrymen had surrounded it. Using crowbars they slowly winched the block onto forty-foot-long skids of beech that rested on soaped wooden crosspieces. It was back-breaking work and painfully slow. First, the men jacked one end of the block onto the skids, then the other. Finally it was loaded and strapped on with rope. Throwing their shoulders into the block, the quarrymen slowly started the stone boat on its downhill journey from the uppermost terrace to the quarry floor. Five men, two on each side and one behind, wrapped lengths of rope strapped to the block around their waists and dug their heels into the steep bank to break the block's descent. As the block slid over the soaped crosspieces, two men shuffled the wooden pieces from back to front. The block came to rest about sixty feet from Frank, slightly above railroad tracks where it would be loaded onto flatbed rail cars to be transported the short distance to the mill.

Frank walked toward the block. It was dirty and muddy from its journey down the mountainside. Its edges were dull and rough, the whole stone nothing more than a giant misshapen, thick-veined, rough mineral.

"What do you have here?" he shouted to the foreman, who was writing on the stone with chalk. The foreman, a short wiry man with a small head and short, powerful arms, was using the chalk to write the name of the quarry, the number of the block, the date and his own initials on the slab. He looked up at Frank, his face creased and sweating.

"It don't look like much now. But wait 'til we polish it," he told Frank in a thick accent.

"This goin' new Indiana statehouse. It don't look like much now, but you wait," he told Frank proudly. "When it cut and polished you see yourself. You wait. This finest vein we ever take out."

Ah, yes, the Indiana statehouse, Frank thought. The job had been nothing but trouble from the start.

Frank remembered the day he told Proctor that the contract had been awarded to Franklin Smith, a small producer in the Midwest.

*

"Smith came in at $160,000," Frank told Proctor.

Proctor was busy at his desk going over correspondence and seemed not to hear.

"On top of that, he promised a delivery schedule a month ahead of ours," Frank continued.

Proctor suddenly put down his pen, rubbed his eyes and stared at Frank.

"I thought you told me we had that bid locked up."

"Brainard, our man in Chicago, told us we did," Frank replied.

"Well then. What happened?"

"John Allen in our Boston office heard from one of the other suppliers that Brainard double-crossed us. Apparently, Smith bribed him to get our bid."

"So Mr. Brainard crossed us?" Proctor repeated. "I wonder what makes him think he can do any better with someone else? Of course, his knowledge of the marble industry was not all that great. Actually, it's a relief to be rid of his continual harping and money complaints. But him and Smith? Now, there's an odd pair. How did those two ever get together?"

"Ever since that Hartford deal, when Smith botched the specs, he's been trying to get into the building trade," Frank replied. "The Indiana statehouse looked like his best shot, but he knew that we were after it, too. That's where Brainard came in."

Proctor stared into space, stroking his beard thoughtfully.

"$160,000," he mused, almost to himself. "It's a ruinous price for him, for anybody. No one's going to make any money on that deal. Still, old Franklin Smith's smarter than I thought. The future is in government building. We shall never see another time when we can produce so large an amount of good marble so cheaply as we did the last few years. Our continued prosperity lies in finding new markets for our product. No Vermont marble has ever been used in this fashion as in the Indiana statehouse, and I am convinced it will be a huge seller."

He suddenly broke off his musing and looked at Frank.

"Send a wire to the Indiana statehouse commission in care of Lewis Whitehead. Tell them our bid was in error. The proper bid should have been $150,000. Send regrets for the error and our hope that it will not detract from our outstanding reputation as the leader in every part of the marble business. Very truly yours, et cetera."

"But sir," Frank could not help interjecting, "you said yourself that $160,000 was too low. Besides, the commissioners have already notified Smith. I hear he has ordered machinery for it and told his supervisor to hire fifty new workers."

"He has? Good. Get that wire out immediately. Tell Whitehead we will begin shipping in March. That's three months ahead of Smith."

What a ridiculous offer! Frank thought as he left Proctor's office. Proctor was taking a money-losing contract on a job he had never done. Why, it would take $5,000 worth of new machinery just to mill the stuff! And then promising delivery in seven months! It seemed sheer financial folly to Frank, and all prompted, it seemed to him, by nothing more than spite against a small company clever enough to outmaneuver him. Frank was sure the bid would be rejected out of hand for coming in after the deadline.

When Frank left his office, Proctor rummaged through his desk. Finding a sheet of paper, he composed another wire in his broad upright script.

"My dear Whitehead," he wrote. "I have just been informed of the error in our bid and am upset and angry that such a large mistake could be made on such a crucial contract. I am sure you were as dumbfounded by our bid as I was. Our original estimate was ridiculously high, and I am informed that because of it, the contract has been temporarily awarded to Franklin Smith. I say 'temporarily' because you did not know our true offer then.

"This letter must be considered confidential, but I think it is in our best interest to speak candidly. Franklin Smith is a fine small company with little experience in filling large orders. He has a small yard but is an aggressive businessman and is trying to build the company up, perhaps too rapidly. They have not the experience they should for the work they are doing. You may recall about a year ago Smith accepted a contract they were not prepared for—a courthouse in Hartford, Connecticut. They bid over their heads and then tried cutting corners to meet the terms. In their haste they misread the specs and delivery fell behind schedule by nearly a month.

"The Indiana statehouse will be the model of the future. Never has so much marble been used in this way, and I can promise you a superior result: more handsome and stronger than any other building marble in the country. It is no secret that the commissioners are anxious to end the delays surrounding this project. I can promise delivery by March, right at the height of the building season. Franklin Smith is a good man, and I would not do or say anything to harm his business, but it is no secret our facilities are much greater than his or any other in the country, and we produce more cheaply. We are experienced at filling large orders and can make our prices very low. This contract means a great deal to us and to our future operations. This must be held in the strictest confidence, but any help by you on our behalf with your colleagues will be generously acknowledged."

*

Except for the freight concessions Proctor had managed to wrangle, the contract had been a financial disaster, Frank thought. The machinery had cost nearly $10,000—twice what they thought—and they had to pay the men overtime to meet the impossible schedule. Now, he was upset because some of the marble they were shipping for the job was too good.

"That's what I want to talk to you about," Frank told the foreman. "We've been shipping much too much good stock. The governor wants to work in as much cheap marble as possible where it will go out of sight and at the same time give a good face."

Just then, a shout and crashing sound came from the other end of the quarry. Frank and the foreman turned. The foreman swore under his breath.

Another stone boat, on the quarry face opposite where this one had been lowered, was being brought down the mountainside. The face was even steeper on that side, and about one hundred feet from the floor, one of the hemp ropes had snapped. At the same time, one of the other brakemen, seeing his neighbor's rope break, stumbled and fell. The two-ton block surged forward off the soaped wooden crosspieces, its skids sliding down the graveled hillside. Only four break men had been taking the rock down, and now the two remaining ones still standing, ropes entwined about their chests and arms, were dragged off their feet and fell onto their faces and chests. The block crashed down the steep quarry face, gaining momentum. It mowed over small brushes and kicked up a storm of dust and debris. Men shouted and jumped out of the way. A horse, in the path of the block and spooked by the commotion, neighed and reared and strained to get free of its harness.

One of the brakemen tried to bounce back onto his feet but tripped and fell forward again. The other two looked like lumpy sacks of potatoes as they were dragged face first down the hillside. A quick-thinking man cut the endangered horse free moments before the stone crashed to a stop near the loading area.

From where he stood, Frank could see the blood on the men's chests and arms and faces as they were turned over.

"Break it up," shouted the foreman, running toward the group of quarry workers who had gathered around the injured men. Two of the men were moaning; the other was still, head turned unnaturally, eyes open and fixed. Blood oozed from the corner of his mouth.

"We must move these men out of here," the foreman said. "You two," pointing to two of the watching quarrymen, "give me hand here. Rest of you—back to work. Nothing you can do. Doctor take care. Let's go, let's go. Break it up. Back to work."

As Frank turned away from the scene, he saw Proctor and another man advancing toward him from the entrance to the quarry floor. He walked over to greet them. The strange man was small and shriveled looking, with sharp features and narrow set eyes, not at all the sort Proctor usually associated with.

"Ahh, Frank, here you are," Proctor said when Frank had reached them. "I want you to meet Mr. Adolphus Smedburg."

So this was Smedburg, Frank thought, sizing up the small diamond merchant's fine clothes. He was considerably overdressed for the June heat with a soft felt hat, topcoat and brown riding gloves.

"Brother Smedburg was once in the pine tar business with Colonel Veazey and myself during the war," Proctor shouted above the noise of the quarry floor.

"How do you do, sir." Frank stuck out his hand.

Smedburg did not take it. Frank withdrew his hand awkwardly, glancing at Proctor.

"The noise and the dirt and commotion of the quarries are hard to take in if you are not used to them," Proctor said to Frank, as if by way of explanation.

Frank turned to Smedburg, but the merchant had not heard a word of what Proctor had said over the commotion of the quarry. Smedburg had a startled, pained look on his face, and his movements were slow and sluggish. He was sweating under his hat. He stared blankly at Proctor, watching his lips move with a confused, bewildered look on his face. Frank remembered the first time he had ventured onto the quarry floor with its ear-splitting explosions of black powder and falling rock, the whistles and curses and shouts of the foremen, the pounding sledgehammers, the frightened screams of men and animals accidently showered by falling rock, the dirt and apparent confusion. He remembered the thumping panic he felt in his chest and head, as if his senses had been cut off. He had trouble thinking, breathing, even swallowing. He had felt like he was suffocating under the din. He knew exactly how Smedburg was feeling. Frank glanced over at Proctor and knew that Proctor knew, too. In fact, he was sure that Proctor had brought Smedburg here for that very purpose.

Proctor later told Frank that, after the war, Smedburg had gone back to New York and his father's diamond business where he had prospered. He had no fond memories of his exile in the army and no close comrades from the war. He avoided reunions and had all but forgotten his contribution to the pine tar deal until the year before his visit to the quarry, when Smedburg read an article in one of the New York papers that Redfield Proctor, "a former Colonel in the Civil War," had been elected governor of Vermont.

Proctor had begun a career in politics several years before. At first, his motive was simply to help advance his business interests. But his gregarious personality and keen interest in his surroundings and genuine love and empathy for people made him a natural politicker. He very likely would have had a political career even with no business interests to promote. He held virtually every elected position in local and state government, beginning as a selectman from Rutland in 1865 and '66. In 1867 and 1868, he represented the town of Rutland in the lower house of the Vermont legislature. In 1874, he moved up to the state senate where he became president pro tempore of that body. In 1876, he was elected lieutenant governor, and two years later, governor.

Proctor brought to the governor's office the same conservative style and fiscal discipline he brought to the management of his own company, advocating reductions in both expenses and taxes.

"Heavy taxation drives away capital and clogs the wheels of business and falls with severest weight on those least able to bear it," he said in his inaugural address.

In addition to passing a strict new divorce law, he succeeded in reducing state expenses, passed a law regulating savings institutions and improved the management of the state prison.

Smedburg sat up when he read the article in the New York paper about the inauguration of Vermont's new governor. The article told how Proctor had nearly died in the conflict, how he had returned to Vermont after the war to open a law practice with another former Union officer, Colonel Wheelock Veazey. It described how Proctor had taken over a small bankrupt marble mill and quickly turned it into a successful enterprise, how he had consolidated all the quarries and mills in the region into "a very large business that shipped marble all over the world."

Although barely elected governor, already, the article said there was wide speculation that Proctor's political ambitions extended far beyond the Vermont capital at Montpelier.

Smedburg put down the paper and decided he should pay a visit to his old army comrade and the new Vermont governor. He recollected that he had never been paid for his services in transporting the "urgent war materials" to Baltimore.

Later that evening, after Proctor had brought Smedburg to the quarry, Proctor discussed Smedburg's visit with Mary in her small sitting room in her comfortable quarters at the Bardwell Hotel in Rutland. Since her first visit to Proctor's office nearly ten years before, Mary's fortunes had improved significantly. Few, other than those most intimately connected to the company, knew the extent of her share or influence in the company. Although not ever mentioned in any company documents, she nevertheless controlled one of the larger blocks of stock in the company, still listed under the name of her late husband, J.J. Myers, and remained one of Proctor's closest confidantes, closer even than Frank and Fletcher. Mary had moved into an elegant townhouse in Washington, D.C., several years ago, largely to accommodate Proctor's more and more frequent business trips to the Capitol. The townhouse on H Street was an ideal arrangement, enabling them to meet discreetly, and Proctor to conduct business. And thanks to Proctor's salesmanship, business in the nation's capital was brisk. No city in the country or the world, for that matter, is so dominated by a single building material as Washington, D.C., is by marble, a stunning memorial to Proctor's enormous influence that lasted long after his death.

In addition to her Washington townhouse, Mary also kept a small suite of rooms at the Bardwell in Rutland, where she and Proctor were now meeting.

Mary wore a tight-fitting, black lace dress that dipped low in the front, emphasizing her breasts, hips and tiny waist. Several strands of pearls hung around her neck. Her hair, thick and lightly streaked with gray, was pulled loosely back from her face and tied at the back of her neck with a red-flowered silk scarf Proctor had bought her on a business trip to San Francisco. Her large blue eyes reflected the glow from the lamp.

"My dear, Mary," Proctor said, holding her hand. "You look lovely this evening."

He kissed her fondly on her forehead. Mary pulled away from him and looked anxiously at him.

"What did that awful man want? Wheelock said something about him coming back to collect on an old war debt, that you and he and Wheelock had been partners in a business venture during the war. Who is he, Redfield? What does he want?"

"Dear Mary," Proctor said, still holding her hand, "ever the businesswoman. You've been away for more than a fortnight. Can't we just sit and talk without spoiling it by talking about Adolphus Smedburg?"

He kissed her hand. "I missed you."

Mary protested, pulling her hand away from him and laughing.

"Business always comes first, Governor Proctor. You are the one who taught me that."

They sat side by side on the sofa, Proctor holding her hands. He sighed, looking at her longingly. Briefly, he told her about Smedburg and the pine tar he had helped Proctor and Veazey smuggle out of Virginia, how after the war Proctor had used the money to buy the farm in Rutland and Veazey the downtown Rutland building where he still practiced law.

"But what does he want now?" Mary asked. "You haven't seen him since the war. What could he possibly want now?"

"Ahh, Mary, come now. What do you think he wants?"

"The newly elected Vermont governor's ear?"

Proctor laughed. "If only that was all he wanted. He can have my ear. He can have both my ears. I'd gladly listen to any political favors he wanted if only I could be sure he would go away."

"Well, then, what does he want? Money?"

"You're getting warmer."

"He's trying to blackmail you?" Mary asked, aghast.

Proctor sighed. "One thing you should always remember about Adolphus Smedburg: he is motivated solely by greed. There is no other aspect to his character whatsoever. He is greed personified. Anger, lust, friendship. He possesses all of these qualities but only as a consequence of greed."

"But Redfield, the war has been over for almost fifteen years. Surely, he can't think you still owe him anything?"

"It's never too late for rascals like Smedburg."

"He's really threatening to blackmail you over something that happened fifteen years ago?"

Proctor smiled tightly at her. "Threatening, my dear. But not succeeding."

"But how can you put him off?" Mary exclaimed, her eyes widening in sudden realization at what he was saying.

"You're the governor of the state! You can't have a story put about by some diamond merchant from New York City, no less, about how you and Wheelock, two Civil War officers and two of the most respected men in the state, smuggled pine tar during the war using Union soldiers and Union rail lines! My God, Redfield, you can't have him saying that! Don't you remember all those stories the opposition put out during the governor's race, criticizing your war record and how you never took part in an active campaign and never were on the firing line?"

"We explained all that during the campaign," Proctor replied impatiently. "My regiment was in reserve at Gettysburg but was not called upon for service."

"Yes, I know, dear," Mary replied, "but you can't have these new stories spread about! You must pay him what he wants! There is no other way. Pay him and get rid of him! My dear, you must be sensible. Don't try to deal with him. Think what is at stake! How can you put him off?"

Proctor stood up and raised her from the sofa as well.

"Greed, my dear, greed. That is how I will put him off."

In the spring of 1879, when Adolphus Smedburg decided to look up his old Civil War comrade and newly elected Vermont governor, the Sutherland Falls Marble Company was at a crossroads. The company Proctor had organized in 1870 had reached its peak capacity. The company was quarrying, milling and shipping all the marble it possibly could from its current holdings. If the company was to expand and profits continue upward, more quarries had to be acquired.

Proctor had long had his eye on the rival Rutland Marble Company, a New York–owned and registered corporation that owned extensive quarries in the Rutland area. In fact, some months before, as a result of Proctor's huge success at Sutherland Falls, the New York stockholders of the Rutland Marble Company had approached him about becoming president of their company. Proctor agreed. But he was president in name only. To actually take control of the company and merge it with his own would take $3 million, a sum even more than Redfield Proctor, with all of his contacts and all of his considerable influence, could muster. But with Smedburg's arrival on the scene, Proctor saw an opportunity to turn a weak attempt at blackmail into a bold grab for empire.

Instead of paying off Smedburg and becoming beholden to him for life, Proctor proposed that Smedburg join him and become a partner in the marble business. He was a natural for the job, Proctor told Smedburg. He was shrewd, a good businessman who recognized opportunity and was not afraid of taking risks. Moreover, the stockholders of the Rutland Marble Company were all from New York. Smedburg was from New York. What better person than Smedburg, a fellow New Yorker, to become treasurer of the new corporation?

By the summer of 1880, the consolidation of the Sutherland Falls Marble Company and the Rutland Marble Company was complete. The cash that Smedburg brought to the deal, combined with the other New York investors, enabled Proctor to merge the two operations and form what would become the largest marble company in the world. The new corporation was called the Vermont Marble Company. Redfield Proctor was president of the corporation, and Adolphus Smedburg, the treasurer.

In order to perform his duties as treasurer, Smedburg insisted that the new company remain incorporated in New York. At first, Proctor was indifferent. The Rutland Marble Company had been a New York corporation, and where a company was actually incorporated made little difference.

"I am not personally particular about the act of incorporation," Proctor wrote Smedburg. "But you are aware that if anything is done one great object of it will be to induce the others (the Rutland Marble Company's New York investors) to join, and they would prefer a Vermont corporation,

A view of the southwest corner of a quarry at the Vermont Marble Company, 1912. *Courtesy of U.S. Geological Survey, copyright Carnkie.*

and of course, would have to be represented on the board, and our law does not require a majority of them to be residents of the state, and requires no returns."

Smedburg relented, and on July 28, 1880, Proctor sent Vermont secretary of state George Nichols the articles of association for forming a corporation under the law of 1874.

"Please return me a certified copy of the corporation papers," Proctor wrote Nichols.

But although Proctor won the incorporation battle, he lost the war. Even though the Vermont Marble Company was indeed a Vermont corporation, and Redfield Proctor its native-born, resident president, the perception that the company was a "foreign" corporation dominated by outside interests, its profits siphoned off by investors from New York City, persisted. Not only was a New York City businessman treasurer of the company, but New York investors constituted more than half of the nine voting trustees. Redfield Proctor may have held controlling interest in the company, but man-for-man, he was outnumbered by the "New York interest."

And that was how Redfield Proctor, who had been born and raised in Vermont, married a Vermonter, raised his children in Vermont, fought and nearly died for Vermont, who was the state's largest landowner, its biggest taxpayer, its most generous philanthropist, *its former governor*, came to be accused of being nothing more than a common carpetbagger, a robber baron, of running a "foreign corporation," a "*New York* corporation" that was now trying to buy a seat in the Vermont legislature.

Yes, of all the charges leveled against Redfield Proctor during the great Rutland town division battle of 1886, Proctor perceived that to be the cruelest cut of all.

Chapter 8

TESTIMONY

Frank left Proctor in his office reading the testimony from the previous day's legislative committee hearing. The *Herald* had been filled with it, and Frank knew Proctor's bad humor would only get worse the more he read. The testimony was shockingly vicious. It was not only the "New York corporation" that opponents went after, they attacked Proctor himself—his company, his motives, his person. None of them had expected this kind of venom.

Frank sighed. The day was going downhill fast. He walked over to his desk and sat down, wondering how long before Proctor summoned him again. He glanced at his timepiece.

I might as well make a stab at getting something accomplished, he reflected.

He opened the middle drawer of his desk and took out a mother-of-pearl-handled pen, a gift from Mrs. Myers, and slipped off the cover. He dipped it into a large, cut glass inkwell on top of his desk. He wrote neatly, "To Mr. Samuel Kerr, in care of the National Press Intelligence."

"Dear Mr. Kerr:" Frank wrote, "I return the draft article of the newspaper story that you sent me and have drawn my pencil through two paragraphs that need to be corrected. 1) Fletcher's wife is from Westford, Vermont, a small town in the northern part of our state. Fletcher and Miss Robinson are quite happily married. He does work in his father's large business as stated, but does not live upon 'the large family estate,' as the governor has no such estate."

If one did not consider a house with nine bedrooms, a music room and library an estate, Frank thought wryly. He continued writing.

"Fletcher owns and occupies a pleasant country home with his wife, to whom he is very devoted, near his father's house and near the business. Contrary to the article, he rarely drinks other than an occasional brandy after dinner."

Frank wrinkled his nose. As if on cue, Fletcher Proctor entered the office.

"Is Father in yet?" he asked, not bothering to greet Frank.

He had on the same clothes he wore the day before. His hair was uncombed, and he had a day-old stubble on his chin. His face was pale and drawn, his boots covered with mud.

"Fletcher! Where have you been? Haven't you been home?" Frank asked.

"That's what I came to tell you. Is Father in?"

"Yes, he's in. He's been here an hour. He wants to see us and Dillingham at nine to talk about our strategy for the legislative vote."

"I can't make it."

"What do you mean you can't make it?"

"The Boys" spoke in low, urgent tones.

"For God's sake, Frank," Fletcher suddenly exploded in a loud whisper. "Just tell him I got tied up. I don't care what you tell him. Tell him anything. Tell him I was playing cards all night. Tell him I got drunk and fell in a ditch. Tell him what you like. It makes no difference to me."

Fletcher turned to leave, swaying slightly.

"Where are you going?" Frank hissed.

Fletcher reached the door, leaning on it as he opened it. He turned around.

"I'm going to go take a piss," he said. "Would you care to join me?"

Just then Proctor called from his office.

"Frank!"

Frank looked toward Proctor's door and back to Fletcher.

"Fraaank," Fletcher mimicked in a low voice, sucking in his stomach, a smirk on his face. "Ohh, Fraa-aank."

Frank clenched his teeth as hard as he could. He longed to open the door to Proctor's office and let him see his son in the flesh, not the phantom Frank constantly covered up for, made excuses for, praised and apologized for. Frank's face was flushed and he was getting sweaty. He knew he was hyperventilating and that any moment Fletcher would notice, too, and start laughing and probably imitate that, too. Frank exhaled as slowly as he could.

"I'll tell your father you were delayed at the mill," Frank said as evenly as he could without breathing. He didn't want to turn toward Proctor's office until Fletcher had left. He and Fletcher stared at one another.

"Frank!" Proctor said again.

The boys could hear him rising and coming toward the door. Fletcher left quickly. Frank exhaled slowly and turned to face Proctor who had just come out of his office.

"I'm sorry," Frank said. "Is there something wrong?"

Proctor had this morning's *Herald* in his hand. His head was down as he stood in the doorway.

"Was someone here?" he asked, looking up.

"Yes. Manny Ruggles from the mill just dropped by. Fletcher sent him to tell you that he's been delayed. There's some sort of problem the foreman needed to discuss with him. He'll be in as soon as he washes up."

Proctor was standing just inside his office. Frank could see the fire had burned low behind him, and he went in and began stirring the ashes to build it up again.

"Thank you," Proctor said. "I can always count on you"—he put just the slightest emphasis on you—"boys to make the right decision. We'll meet this afternoon. I can see from reading this testimony that we have a bigger fight on our hands than I had bargained for."

Frank, still shaking from his encounter with Fletcher, kept his back to Proctor. He continued to fuss with the fire.

"You were right," Proctor continued.

Frank stood up. Proctor waved the transcript at him.

"We left too early," he said. "Compared to some of these others, Dorr sounds almost pleasant. I can't believe some of this. Listen to this one."

Proctor read from the newspaper: "'Some fellows, about as wise as the man who burned down his barn to get rid of the rats, propose to divide this grand old town simply because the town hall is too small.'"

Proctor smiled at Frank. "You're the literary man," he said. "Is that what you call mixed metaphors?"

Frank laughed. "I believe that was Henry Dyer. I think he is just mixed up."

This time Proctor laughed. He read again. "'Division is unjust, uncalled for and undemocratic.'"

"I like that," he said. "It's uncommonly rhythmic."

Frank laughed again. *How I adore this man!* he thought, forgetting Fletcher as he listened to Proctor read.

"'It is the work of ages to make a large town. You have no place nor material to make another like Rutland.'"

"'Rutland divided would pass from first class to third rate.

"'I have no doubt dismemberment…'" Proctor paused over the word. "'…Dismemberment of Rutland would depreciate all real estate in view of necessarily increased taxation to support three towns instead of one.

"'This project has been advanced with great skill and adroitness, but bottom facts show it is only special favor to the few at the expense of the many.

"'Division is nothing more than the shrewd work of Governor Proctor and his able counsel.

"'I cannot conceive of any necessity for division.

"'I am bitterly opposed to division and know of no reason for it.

"'To divide the town would be a great injury to it.

"'Division of Rutland into three towns would increase aggregate town expenses very largely.

"'The smallness of the town hall is a good reason for building a new one, not for dividing the town. We will then have to build three town halls. Doesn't Governor Proctor know anything about math?'"

Proctor chuckled. He read on.

"'I am not in favor of division. I am not in favor of a city charter. I am not in favor of any change. Leave things as they are.

"'Rutland should not be divided.

"'Division would take away a very considerable source of taxes that are jointly the property of all the citizens of the town.

"'Division would leave Proctor and West Rutland with all the town's marble deposits at the expense of Rutland itself.

"'The present bills before the House are uncalled for.

"'It is wrong and unjustified to set off a small portion of the town to perpetuate the name of a single individual, whose only purpose is to perpetuate his name and regulate his own taxation.

"'It is not necessary, best or proper to divide this town.

"'In union there is strength, and division will hurt all the inhabitants.

"'Division would be injurious, and the people don't want it. The legislature should get the sentiments of the people through a vote on the measure. Then they would see.

"'I'm a farmer and I don't know of any farmer who is not opposed to division.

"'I'm a businessman and I don't know of any of my customers who are not opposed to division.

"'Division would be injurious and hurt the entire region.

"'Division would be injurious to the best interest of the town.

"'Division would be injurious to the people of the town.'"

Proctor's voice had risen and fallen as he read the testimony. He looked up at Frank.

"You say there was even more?"

"Yes, it went on and on, very repetitious. What was most noteworthy were not the arguments but the numbers."

"Yes, yes," Proctor agreed. "But I don't like this argument for a vote of the people. How many repeated that sentiment?"

"As I recall, perhaps one or two others. There was one testimony, in particular, on that subject that I singled out for you."

"Which is that?"

Frank went over to Proctor's desk and found a separate transcript.

"A fellow named Patch," Frank said.

"Patch? Do I know him?"

"J.C. Patch," Frank replied, reading his notes. "Age sixty-seven. Said he has lived in Proctor for twenty years."

"Patch, of course. He's a builder. I know him. He's a good carpenter. He's done quite a bit of work for us. His son works for the company, too, I believe."

"Two of his sons do," Frank replied.

"He testified? What did he say?"

"He said he didn't think division was necessary, best or proper for the town."

Proctor grunted. "Original thoughts."

"He also said he didn't think a fair expression of opinion about division could be secured in Proctor without a secret vote, and if that were to happen, he said that at least three-quarters of the people would vote to oppose division. But without a secret vote, he said people in Proctor were afraid to sign petitions or speak openly against division because they were afraid that such a move would bring down the heavy hand of their employer."

"Are those his exact words?"

"Yes."

"Heavy hand of their employer?" Proctor repeated.

"Yes. So then Mansur, a member of the committee, asked Patch if he knew of any class of working people that lived more comfortably or were apparently more thriving than those in Proctor."

Proctor nodded. "Who asked him that? Mansur?"

"Yes, from Brighton."

"Make sure he knows I know he asked that question," Proctor said. "What did Patch say?"

Frank looked at his notes again.

"He replied that he knew of no working men anywhere who got less wages, who paid more rent or who worked longer or in harder conditions."

Chapter 9

FACTS

When William P. Dillingham, acting as counsel on behalf of former governor Redfield Proctor, submitted a request to the Vermont legislature in September 1886 to divide the Town of Rutland, Vermont, into thirds, Rutland was the largest, most populous and richest town in the state.

"I don't know about this, Redfield," Dillingham said, looking over the division petition. "The richest town in the state. You're going to make a lot of enemies over this one."

Dillingham, Proctor, Frank and Fletcher were in the library in Proctor's estate (yes, it really was an estate). The room was large with expensive wall coverings and a thick wool rug in front of the fireplace. Opposite the fireplace on the south wall, three large windows filtered slanting beams of sunlight through heavy drapes. Shelves filled with leather-bound books lined the other walls. The room was richly furnished with heavy tapestried chairs. An oak table with four chairs took up the center of the room. Dillingham and Frank sat across from each other at this table. Fletcher was stretched out in one of the nearby chairs.

"It can't be helped," Proctor said from the doorway. "We need to act now. We have only a short window of opportunity before the next general election. Everything must be perfect. There must be no mistakes in our petition."

"There won't be," Dillingham replied, looking up earnestly at Proctor. He was eleven years younger than Proctor and had a quick, boyish grin and smooth face that made him seem more a contemporary of Frank and Fletcher; he led many of his opponents to dismiss him as too wet behind the ears and innocent to play hardball. But Dillingham was a brilliant lawyer and nearly as flawless an actor. The son of Vermont's first post–Civil War governor, Dillingham's best role was as the slightly awestruck, deferential young lawyer. It was a part he was perfectly typecast for, and the performance (and his meticulous homework, which often went unnoticed) won him raves and waves of decisions and the respect and admiration of his colleagues, as well as his opponents.

"I'll leave you gentlemen to work out the details," Proctor continued, turning to leave. He shut the door behind him.

"Yes, sir," Dillingham replied. He turned his attention back to the papers on the table in front of him.

"Let's see," he mused, reading from the top sheet. "Rutland was originally chartered in 1751."

He made a small correction on the page. "It has an area of thirty square miles."

He looked up at Frank and Fletcher. "That makes it the largest town in the state."

Frank nodded, listening intently.

Dillingham turned over the page and continued reading.

"It has a population of sixteen thousand, which is also the largest in the state."

He turned over another sheet.

"And with a grand list of $105,010, it's also the wealthiest town in the state."

"Actually, that's not true," Fletcher yawned from his chair.

Dillingham looked at Fletcher. "What do you mean? Rutland's grand list is way over that of any other town. I have the figures right here."

"Yeah, but $90,000 of Rutland's grand list is owned by the Vermont Marble Company, father's personal property and me. *We* are the richest town in the state."

No one said anything.

"Actually," Frank finally broke in. "You and your father and the company are assessed for about $86,000, not $90,000."

"$86,392.82 to be exact," Dillingham said.

"Eighty-six, ninety, it's still more than four-fifths of Rutland's total grand list and more than any other town in the state," Fletcher replied. He smirked at Frank. "I can do math, you know."

He turned back to Dillingham. "I would say we own this town."

"That may be true," Dillingham replied judiciously. "But I don't think that should be our main argument. You and your father might own most of this town and pay by far the most taxes, but there are sixteen thousand other residents in this town. We need to bring them 'round to our position. Flaunting your wealth is not the way to do it. If this matter were ever put to a popular vote, you'd lose, hands down, no matter how much money you have or taxes that you might pay."

"I think the size of the town hall remains our strongest argument," Frank said. "Its capacity is only 1,500, which is much too small for a town the size of Rutland. Not all the voters can fit in the hall at any one time. And even if you open up the galleries the capacity is still only 2,000, still woefully short of the total registered voters in the town."

"Yes, that's right," Dillingham nodded. "We will argue that the town has outgrown its government."

"The size of the town hall is really irrelevant," Fletcher remarked. "The highest-ever recorded turnout for a town meeting up to now was only 1,200, which easily fits into the hall the way it is." He looked at Frank. "You don't even have to open up the galleries."

"Thank you Fletcher," Dillingham said, his voice tinged with just a hint of sarcasm. "That may be true, but it's not the point we want to make. It doesn't matter if the biggest turnout in the past has been only 1,200. The point is the town hall is too small to hold all the town's voters."

"You know," Frank added thoughtfully. "Even if you cut out the voters from Proctor and West Rutland, that old town hall is still too small to hold the remaining voters in Rutland."

Dillingham sighed. "Yes, I know."

He looked at Frank. "We need to keep the argument away from that fact. The most important thing is to stress the present. Rutland has outgrown its government, period. And the proof is the town hall. It's way too small to hold all the voters in the town on Town Meeting Day."

"How many signatures did the opposition gather against division?" Frank asked.

"They turned in a total of 2,085."

"Whew! Did you challenge them?" Frank asked.

"Absolutely. We found several hundred were either dead, duplicates or nonresidents of Rutland."

"So how many were left?"

The railroad was instrumental in the rapid growth of the Vermont Marble Company during the late 1800s and early 1900s. *Courtesy Vermont Historical Society.*

"1,340."

"Jeez," Fletcher broke in again from his chair. "That's still more than have ever turned out for a town meeting. The largest turnout for a town meeting was 1,200."

Frank looked at Dillingham in exasperation. It was as if Fletcher knew this one fact and was trying to impress them by inserting it into the conversation whenever he could.

"Where did the signatories come from?" Frank asked.

"What do you mean?" Dillingham replied. "They're all Rutland residents. We threw out all the nonresidents."

"Yes, but what part of Rutland?"

"I see what you mean." Dillingham checked his papers. "Of the 1,340 legitimate voters who signed petitions against division, 53 live in West Rutland."

"What about Proctor?" Frank asked.

"One."

Chapter 10

DORRS

It galls me to think Redfield is going to get away with his neat little grab for power," Seneca Dorr said irritably.

"How can you be so sure?" his wife answered absently, not bothering to look up from the papers she was reading.

"Ha!" Dorr snorted. "Have you ever known Redfield not to get anything he sets his sights on?"

Julia Caroline Ripley Dorr, or J.C.R. Dorr, as the readers of her poetry knew her, and Seneca Dorr sat at the large, rough-hewn maple kitchen table in their house in Center Rutland. As Julia turned over one of the pages in front of her, she flashed back to that memory when they had first settled on the name for the house.

*

"The Maples," Julia had insisted more than thirty years before when they broke ground for the large, rambling house situated on a gentle knoll above the west bank of the Otter Creek.

"We must call it 'The Maples,' Seneca."

Julia ran happily around the hilltop field, stopping every few steps to exclaim over the view of the mountains to the east, the babbling of the river as it curved lazily through their property and the stately line of century-old sugar maples that lined both sides of the nearly overgrown logging road up the knoll.

"And here, Seneca, here is where the kitchen must be, with large windows looking east to Mount Killington."

Julia stood by a patch of daisies, her long hair swept loosely back from her face with a scarf. A balmy spring breeze blew loosened strands about her face. Even then, although not yet thirty-five, Julia's once jet black hair was already heavily streaked with white. As she laughed and danced and stooped to pick him a buttercup, Seneca watched his wife with an amused grin.

"Now let me see your chin," she told him with mock seriousness. "I'm afraid, sir, that beard has got to go." She tickled his neck and face with the flower.

Chuckling and ducking his head, Dorr caught Julia's arm in midair and pulled her to him, kissing her on the lips. They fell to the ground, laughing.

*

"If Redfield wants something he just goes ahead and takes it, and everyone else be damned," Dorr continued irritably, interrupting Julia's reverie. "He'll ruin this town but that's no concern to him. His only concern is money and power."

"But what about your speech, dear?"

Julia looked up at her husband across from her. Her lips were pursed in concentration, her pen poised, ready to mark passages she particularly liked. Her longtime friend, Louisa May Alcott, was coming up from Boston this afternoon for the meeting of the Fortnightly Society that evening, and Julia, who had first met Alcott and her father, Bronson Alcott, at Ralph Emerson's house in Concord, Massachusetts, nearly a quarter century ago, was reading over a poem Frank Partridge had written in Alcott's honor. Julia looked at her husband scowling at his plate across from her. Impetuously, she rose from her chair, putting down her pen and Frank's poem in a jumble on the table. She hurried around the table and knelt beside him.

"You mustn't let Redfield upset you so, darling," she told him soothingly, rubbing his cheek with her finger.

"Ha! That bastard!" Dorr shot back.

The years had been hard on Seneca Milo Dorr. Sometimes, even Julia found herself looking at him and wondering what had happened to the handsome, socially connected, bright young man she had married, to the earnestness and fire that emanated from him and had first attracted her to him, to the promises he had never kept. Everything had seemed possible then for Seneca Dorr. His passion was politics, and he might have gone a long way with his good looks and oratorical gifts. But in the end, his instincts were all wrong.

His first mistake was turning his back on his friend, neighbor and benefactor, former president Martin Van Buren. Van Buren lived next to the Dorrs in Ghent, New York, and had taken considerable pains with Dorr, confiding in him, introducing him to all the right people. When Dorr suddenly bolted the Democrats in 1856 to take the stump for Charles Fremont, the Republican Party's first presidential candidate, Van Buren was considerably irked. He blackballed Dorr. And when Fremont lost the election, Dorr was out of power with his new party as well.

Dorr's second mistake was encouraging his wife's silly little writings. At first, it seemed to Dorr a harmless pastime that helped ease Julia's homesickness for her large family and home in Rutland, Vermont. Dorr even secretly sent two of Julia's poems that he found hidden in one of his law books in the library to the *Columbian Magazine*. The delight on Julia's face when she received a letter of acceptance and a check for five dollars overshadowed her embarrassment at being discovered by her husband.

For his part, Dorr, though surprised and perhaps just a twinge jealous at this easy success, nevertheless felt a genuine sense of pride. He continued to encourage Julia to write and send her poems to publishers and magazines. He even took over some of the minding of their three small children so she could write more.

But somewhere the line between homesick outlet and literary career was crossed. Julia's poems began to be published more and more often and in bigger and more prestigious magazines and journals. Shunned by Van Buren and his old associates, Dorr's own law practice began to decline even as his wife's literary career was taking off. He took over more of the household responsibilities so Julia could sally forth to meet with publishers and editors, lecture before groups, attend parties and literary meetings, chair committees. His shy, self-conscious wife had blossomed into one of the leading literary figures of the day, and Dorr, his own political career fizzing rapidly, more and more was left in the shadows.

Dorr's biggest error, however, was moving back to Rutland. It was supposed to be just a visit with Julia's family before the Dorrs moved west to try and start over again following Fremont's defeat. But the outpouring of affection that the boisterous, competitive, successful, respected and above all, close-knit Ripley clan showered upon them overwhelmed Julia. Although Dorr had his doubts, he was no match for Julia's six half brothers and sisters and their families.

Bowing to Julia's entreaties, in 1856 he sold their large, fine house in Ghent with its barns and former slave quarters in the rear and bought a parcel of land less than a mile upstream from "The Center," the Ripley homestead. In time, the two covered bridges that crossed Otter Creek between The Center and The Maples became known as the Ripley Bridge and the Dorr Bridge.

Dorr's misgivings about settling in the Ripley shadow in Rutland were borne out all too soon. His own father had died when he was four, and Seneca had grown up in an all-female household, spoiled by his mother and sisters. He was unused to the pranks and the hard-driven, competitive work ethic to succeed and to lead that characterized the Ripley men. No matter how hard Julia tried to include him in the family, Dorr always felt like an outsider. One business failure after another followed. Everything the Ripleys were good at—farming, marble, community service—Dorr was a miserable failure at.

Losing the Sutherland Falls marble mill was the hardest to take. Dorr knew he had been outmaneuvered by Proctor and Mary Myers and watched their success bitterly. The fact that much of the Ripley money originally came from marbling, a business the family continued to operate in Center Rutland, only inflamed his bitterness. Adding insult to injury was Proctor's political success. Proctor and his many friends and associates, including some of Julia's half brothers, ran the Republican Party, which at that time was the equivalent of running the state. Frustrated and bitter in the end, Dorr sought his own political and personal identity in extreme causes, taking immense secret pleasure at the embarrassment he caused his wife's oh-so-proper family.

Julia looked longingly at her husband, smoothing the scowl on his face with her finger. His frown only deepened.

"But what about your speech, dear?" she repeated. "Cornelia told me it was a wonderful speech. All the men were talking about it. And what about all of the other testimony that has been given in opposition to the division proposal? And the letters and the petitions?" Julia continued. "Surely the legislature cannot go against the wishes of the people. And sentiment against division is near universal. I haven't seen this town so united since the Confederates fired on Fort Sumter. Why, I don't think I've heard or read a single word in favor of the proposal except, of course, from Redfield and his cronies."

"You've talked to Cornelia, but you obviously haven't talked to her husband, William, lately."

"What do you mean?" Julia answered, frowning in dismay.

"Just what I said. You obviously have not talked to your brother, William, lately."

Dorr abruptly rose from the table, knocking his chair over. He stooped clumsily to retrieve it, bending awkwardly, his stomach in the way. His face flushed with the effort and his anger. He shoved the chair roughly back under the table, scraping the wide maple planks of the kitchen floor loudly.

"I never thought the Ripleys would sell out their town and their children for money," Dorr said. "I'm just glad your father isn't alive to see it. The high and mighty Ripleys and their precious honor and military commissions don't mean a thing when it comes to the almighty dollar!"

Dorr stormed from the room.

"Seneca, dear. Whatever do you mean?" Julia called after him. "What has William done to upset you so?"

Julia called after her husband to no avail. She stood uncertainly in the middle of the kitchen looking after him.

Chapter 11

W.Y.W.

General William Young Warren Ripley rarely smiled.

Emotions, his father, William Young Ripley, had taught him a long time ago, were useless. They don't change anything, solve anything or mean anything. They only clutter a man's thinking. Emotions are better left to women.

William could not get his thoughts off his father this morning.

"Times change, Father," he muttered irritably to himself as he padded softly downstairs in the early morning darkness, shivering in spite of his heavy wool shirt in the cold of the still house.

William Young Ripley, the father, had been dead more than ten years, but William Young Warren Ripley, the son, could feel his father's heavy presence throughout The Center more keenly this morning than if his father was still waiting for him in the kitchen for their ritual morning coffee and series of grunts and abrupt sentences that passed for communication between them. In his whole life, William Young Warren Ripley had never managed to get into the kitchen in the morning before his father.

*

"Were you scared?" his father asked him, putting a stern mask over the fright he had felt as he watched young William galloping wildly across the field on the old plow horse.

"No, sir," eight-year-old William told his father manfully. "She would've thrown me if I'd been scared."

William held the reins of the mare carelessly in his left hand as he slipped deftly off her back onto the ground. His knees buckled as he hit the ground, and William could feel the blood rushing from his face as he staggered and half fainted into his father's arms. For a moment, William Young Ripley held his son tightly. As his head slowly stopped spinning, young William was aware of the pounding of his father's heart. His father released him abruptly, standing young William up brusquely.

"You were a very brave young man today, William."

William's father turned abruptly on his heel back toward the barn.

"Now if you have finished racing Tristram around like some Thoroughbred racehorse, you can get back to plowing," he said over his shoulder. "I expect this field to be finished before suppertime."

*

General W.Y.W. Ripley had inherited every ounce of his father's aloofness, work habits, commanding presence and half of the family marble fortune. The other half had gone to his younger brother, General Edward Hastings Ripley.

Generally speaking, however, the two brothers had inherited none of their father's shrewdness. Younger brother Ned, a genuine war hero, was something of a dilettante and lady killer, a "cosmopolite," as his half sister, Julia Ripley Dorr, liked to describe him. He was not interested in returning to Rutland after the war to manage the marble business and generously entrusted his share and interests in the family business to his older brother, William, to manage. Ned loved action and women and left for New York City in pursuit of both.

So when William visited his younger brother in the city to tell him he was planning to sell the business, Ned agreed wholeheartedly.

"It's a terrible burden," Ned told William, nodding his head sympathetically. "There's a lot of money to be made today. Easy money. A lot easier than in marble."

"Father started this business from nothing and made a great fortune out of it," William rebuked his brother. "Marble gave you everything you wanted as a child and later as an adult."

"I'm not saying we were poor, William. All I'm saying is that I agree with you. I think maybe it's time to sell and get out from under Father's shadow. Marble was good for Father, no one's disputing that. All I'm saying is that maybe it's not so good for his sons. As long as you remain in marble, it will always be Father's business, no matter how long he's been dead. Lord knows I loved him as much as you did. But maybe it's time you found your own niche, just as I have found my own niche, my own reputation and my own money here in New York. For God's sake, William! I thought you came here to get my permission to sell, not my opposition. I'm giving you my permission and my blessing."

The truth of it is: I'm just not the man you were, Father, William thought darkly to himself as he stoked the fire in the kitchen. *Or even you, Ned. We may both be generals, but everyone knows you are the true war hero. You are the one who rode his horse into battle.*

William scowled darkly. He was a tall, erect man with piercing blue eyes, heavy brows and thick, wavy dark hair that he wore long, disguising a receding hairline. Like all the members of the Ripley family, his hair was prematurely streaked with white. He had a large, straight nose and a pasty, pock-marked complexion. A heavy beard disguised thick lips but could not hide the frown that characterized his features.

"Who is that cross-looking boy over there?" Cornelia Thomas had asked her best friend, Mary Ripley, one day in school.

"That's my older brother, William," Mary replied.

No one ever called him anything but William. His very countenance seemed to discourage nicknames. But Cornelia Thomas sensed something deeper in William than most women. She schemed with her friend, Mary, to introduce them and married him a few years later. Cornelia softened him, but he let few but her ever see that side of him.

General W.Y.W. Ripley had few close friends but had the respect of everyone he met. His bearing and natural leadership qualities invariably cast him in a position of power, but he shunned political office. In this respect, too, as in so many others, he was like his father.

But somehow William knew he was not behaving on this day as his father would have. His father bent to no man. His father would never allow himself to be compromised or bribed. Of this, his son and namesake, William Young Warren Ripley, was certain.

Chapter 12

Bribe

"General, come in, come in. It's good to see you."

Proctor came out to the small waiting room outside his office in Center Rutland and greeted General William Young Warren Ripley warmly, shaking hands and clapping him on the shoulder.

"How was your fishing trip to Maine?" Proctor asked. "Veazey and I just got back from a big moose hunting trip to northern Maine the last two weeks of September. I sure hope your trip was better than ours. Ours was a disaster. It was very cold, stormy, and the ice was half an inch thick. It was snowing so hard the moose and caribou were all back in the thickets away from the water. We saw no game, nothing but a small black bear about thirty feet away, and he was more frightened than I was and got out of the way before I could even raise my rifle."

Proctor laughed. "Come on in and tell me about your trip. Were the fish biting?"

"And then some," replied the general as the men entered Proctor's office. Proctor shut the door.

"It was a very profitable expedition," Ripley continued. "The weather was quite pleasant, and the fish exceedingly obliging."

Proctor laughed again. "Wonderful. Some of the best tasting trout I have ever eaten I've caught on fishing trips to Maine. A couple of years ago, I think I broke the record by hooking seventeen in three hours. I had two rods and would turn one over to a helper to land after playing the fish a little and then take up the other rod and hook another."

"Do you mind if I smoke?" Ripley asked.

"Not at all. Here, try one of these." Proctor got up to offer Ripley a box of cigars from a side table. "President Cleveland gave me these the last time I saw him."

The general selected one of the cigars and settled back in his chair. Proctor put the box back on the table.

"I trust you are ready to support the party at the next election?" he asked Ripley, settling into the chair opposite his guest.

"Of course, Redfield. You know me, ready to make a speech anytime, whether I'm asked or not."

The two men laughed.

"That's very generous of you, William. Heh, heh," Proctor chuckled again.

The room was furnished simply—almost spartan. At one end was an enormous heavy wooden desk in front of a bay window on the wall opposite the door. Proctor had put away the papers and legislative committee testimony from this morning's *Herald*, and the top of the desk was now barren. The only thing on it was a heavy black telephone, one of the first in Rutland. A straight-backed chair faced the desk for Proctor's recording secretary. In front of the fireplace on the side wall was a camelback horsehair couch flanked by two overstuffed chairs. Proctor and Ripley sat facing each other in these two chairs. A wool scatter rug covered the parquet floor in front of the fireplace. No pictures broke up the drab, colorless walls.

"William, I'm going to get right to the point," Proctor said, shifting in his chair.

"You always do, Redfield."

"We are engaged in a terrible fight over this division issue, much bigger than I had anticipated. It would help our cause tremendously to have your public support. Your father was a very respected man in this town, as is your entire family. People trust you, William. They listen to you. Right now, sentiment against division is running so strong that, frankly, I'm worried. It hasn't turned ugly yet, but with young Percy Clement printing his inflammatory rhetoric and outright lies every day in the *Herald*, things are getting out of hand. Today, he had the gall to print that more than half the names on our petitions were false, dead or duplicates. Sometimes I wonder why we went to war when somebody can print such outright lies in the name of free speech! But the charge that really gets me is this 'political boss' thing. It's dangerous, William. I could crush them all faster than any stone crusher right now. I certainly do not need to divide the town for any personal political gain. You know that. That's preposterous! But the rhetoric is getting so inflammatory and the charges so out of hand, we've lost touch with the reason behind division. The town has just gotten too big and too prosperous to be properly governed as it is. That's the only reason behind this movement to divide the town. You know that. But that very simple fact has gotten lost amid all these personal attacks and lies and all this nonsense about a 'political boss.' Frankly, things are getting so ugly that I am starting to get concerned about violence. This issue will end, and we must all pick up the pieces and get back to living together. I am afraid relations may be permanently damaged by this fight."

"I agree with you," Ripley replied. "I, too, am concerned at the venom this issue has generated and all of the personal attacks. But I really don't see what I can do. You know my position."

"William, you sell yourself short. Appeal to the opposition. Reason with them. You know what's right for the town. You know division is the only way to have an orderly and fair government. You know division is the only way for us to continue to prosper and grow. I appeal to you as a fellow officer and a Republican. Please use your influence and your family's standing to bring some wisdom and dignity to this fight."

"You give me far too much credit."

"Not at all. You are a very persuasive and well-respected man, as is your entire family. You are probably the most honorable man in Rutland. If you support this proposal, it must be the right thing to do. I want to show that all the leading citizens of the town support our position."

"What about Clement?"

"What about him?" Proctor replied dismissively. "He's a hot head, that's all—hardly a man to look up to. You, on the other hand, are one of the leaders of this town. You would never do anything to harm Rutland. Everyone knows that. Your family has deep roots here. People look up to you, including me."

Proctor looked up at the general and smiled warmly at him.

"I'd like to help you out, Redfield. But I'm afraid that on this issue, we are on opposite sides. The only appeal I am going to make is for you to withdraw this petition. I'm already scheduled to go before the legislative committee tomorrow morning and state the case for the opposition. I'm surprised your friends on the committee didn't tell you that."

"Actually, they did," Proctor said quietly. "I asked you here today in the hopes of convincing you to change your testimony or, at the very least, not to testify at all."

"I'm sorry, Redfield. I can't do that. My father loved this town. He made a fortune here, raised his family here, is buried here. This is a great town, the greatest town in the state. What you are doing is wrong. You divide this town and you'll ruin it. I feel very strongly on this issue. And I plan to oppose you with everything I have. I'm sorry."

Ripley stubbed out his cigar and stood up to leave.

"Not as sorry as I am, General."

Ripley glanced at Proctor, surprised at the use of his title.

Proctor looked soberly at Ripley. "We have been friends a long time," he said. "I would hate to see this issue divide us."

"Then withdraw your petition."

"That is not possible."

"Then we have nothing more to discuss."

"Sit down, General," Proctor repeated. "I have something to say to you that I think you will find very interesting."

Ripley drew himself up to his full six feet, one and one-half inches.

"Our conversation has ended," he said stiffly. "Good day, Redfield."

"Just a minute, General."

Ripley turned toward the door.

"Your father did, indeed, make a fortune in this town. No doubt," Proctor said. "He was a shrewd man—a good businessman. I admired him greatly."

Ripley said nothing. He walked toward the door.

"But it is no secret that the Ripley fortune has all but disappeared," Proctor continued.

"What do you know?" Ripley replied tersely.

"I know enough to know that the fortune your father made is nearly gone."

"My finances and my family's finances are of no concern to you. You don't know what you are talking about."

"Oh no?"

"No, you don't." Ripley turned again to leave.

"I know that every bank in town has denied you credit. I know your marble operation is losing money. I know you need to make serious investments in your equipment and machinery, but none of the local banks will support you.

The banks here have bankrolled you for a long time, mostly on the strength of the Ripley name. I know they have denied you any more extensions."

"So?" Ripley said defensively. "We'll get the money we need. Our quarries still have a lot of marble left. The vein we're working now is one of the richest we have ever taken out."

"Yes, but you need to make investment in new equipment to get at it. Your father continually reinvested into the operation. But you and your brother, Ned, have seriously neglected a lot of your machinery and other maintenance. I know for a fact that you have only two operating cranes, and they are seriously dated."

"Is there a point to this?"

Ripley had stopped near the door and faced Proctor defiantly, his face flushed. He pursed his lips.

"What if we do need some new equipment?" he continued. "What concern is that of yours?"

"I'd like to help you out."

"Right," Ripley said disdainfully. "I know what kind of help you propose: my testimony for a loan. Well, the answer is no."

Proctor laughed shortly. "Hardly. Why would I give you a loan when none of the banks will? The problem is collateral. You don't have sufficient collateral for a loan. Not even your testimony is enough collateral for a loan."

"This conversation is over. I am not going to stand here and let you insult me or my family. I'll see you at the committee hearing tomorrow."

Ripley turned abruptly on his heel.

"Just a minute, General," Proctor said, using Ripley's title again. "Sit down. You're right, I want your testimony. But I am not going to give you a loan for it."

"Then what?"

"I have a straight-up business proposition for you."

"And what might that be?"

"I'd like to buy your operation."

"It's not for sale."

"No?"

"No. It's not for sale. Not to you or anyone else. My father started this company, and his sons are not going to sell him out."

"His sons?" Proctor raised his eyebrows. "You're the only son in the business. Ned's off in New York. What has he done lately for the company except spend his inheritance?"

"Leave my brother out of this."

"Listen, William," Proctor leaned forward. "The company's floundering. I know it is, and so do you. And no bank will support you. What kind of legacy is bankruptcy for your father? Think of your family's standing in this community. Imagine what bankruptcy would do to your family; their honor; your half sister, Julia Dorr, and her literary reputation and career. Do you really want to do that to your family? To your father's memory?"

"The company is a long ways from bankruptcy."

"It's closer than you think. I know you lost that contract for the new bank building in Boston. That was going to be your salvation, the collateral you promised the banks. But there is no contract."

Ripley staggered slightly in surprise. "How do you know that?"

"Because we won the contract."

"Impossible. We had the low bid."

"And we had the lower bid."

Ripley glared at him. "And who did you bribe to get that?"

Proctor smiled tightly. "I resent your accusation, General."

"And I resent this conversation, Colonel." Ripley turned again to the door.

"So now that you have lost that contract, once again, you have no collateral," Proctor continued.

"We'll get the money. We've got a lot of marble deposits."

"And no way to get them."

"We'll get the money," Ripley repeated.

"Actually, you're right. You will get the money," Proctor said. "Tomorrow morning, you will receive an offer of $275,000 for the Ripley and Sons Marble Company, all real estate, equipment and stock."

"That's preposterous!" Ripley exclaimed. "The company's got to be worth nearly twice that."

"In its present condition? I don't think so. You've greatly neglected the physical property. There are several liens on the property. If you inquire around, I think you will find that $275,000 is a very generous offer."

Ripley flushed. "If it's so generous, then why are you making it?"

"Because you are my friend."

Ripley said nothing.

"Because, as you point out," Proctor continued, "there are significant deposits of good quality marble there. It will take a very large investment to get them out. But I'm willing to take that risk to help out a friend."

"Some risk at $275,000!" Ripley muttered, his teeth clenched in anger.

"$275,000 is the only offer I'm going to make. You can take it or not."

"And if I don't?"

Proctor looked soberly at his friend. "Be serious, William. Is bankruptcy really the legacy you want for your father? His sons? Your family? You lost that contract. That was your last hope. I'm throwing you a lifeline. When you think about it, you will see that $275,000 is really a very fair price, especially considering the condition of the property and the liens on it."

"But the marble deposits…"

"Are worthless if you can't quarry them. And right now, you can't quarry them."

"What if I don't make this deal?"

"You'll make it."

"How can you be so sure?"

"Because I know you, and I knew your father before you, and you are just like your father. Your father would have made this deal, and you will, too."

"Leave my father out of this."

"Very well."

Proctor stood up and walked around to his desk. Ripley scowled. He was silent. Proctor stood behind his desk, staring thoughtfully at him.

"$275,000?" Ripley finally asked in a strained voice.

Proctor smiled sadly. "Yes," he nodded. "$275,000."

"How do I know you won't renege on this somehow?"

"General, you insult me and our long friendship."

"And your offer insults me!" Ripley replied angrily.

"Then I guess we are even." Proctor was silent for several seconds. "William, we have been friends for a long time," he finally said in a quiet voice. "This is a legitimate business transaction. I offered you a fair price for your business, a very fair price, one you would not get anywhere else, I dare say. You will either take it or not. It is totally up to you."

"I still want to know what assurances I have that if I agree to this price, you will indeed carry out your end of the transaction."

"It's all right here." Proctor opened his desk drawer and pulled out a stack of papers. "Here." He proffered them to Ripley. "If you examine them, you will see that everything is in order."

"I don't want them," Ripley growled.

A view of one of the quarries at the Vermont Marble Company, likely taken between 1900 and 1906. *Courtesy Library of Congress, from the collection of the Detroit Publishing Company, 1880–1920.*

"Very well." Proctor put the papers back in his desk drawer, closed it and faced his friend.

"You have my word as a fellow officer that you will receive a note in full for $275,000, drawn on my personal account and made out to you, for the Ripley and Sons marble company, all real estate, equipment and stock, tomorrow afternoon."

Proctor paused.

"Right after you finish giving your testimony before the committee—in favor of division."

Chapter 13

MOTIVE

"The politics of division are embarrassingly simple."

Frank wrote neatly and carefully in his journal, pausing over the word "embarrassingly." He formed his letters sparingly, upright, with tight curls on the descenders. He thought for a minute and scratched out "embarrassingly" and wrote "very" over it, remembering Julia Dorr's admonition to him to write simply and clearly, eschewing the use of flowery language when simple words would do.

"The politics, of course, have to do with power, or rather the erosion of power," Frank continued. "It's hard to believe, but Redfield is losing control. He recognizes this fact himself, although he has a mistaken view of who the enemy is. Redfield thinks he is losing control to a group of men, that he can simply divide and conquer them. The problem is the enemy is not that easily defined. A single man, a group of men—that is indeed an easy contest for him. No," Frank mused, his pen scratching hurriedly to keep up with the dramatic swell of his thoughts. "Redfield is losing control to the inexorable forces of history. Can even Redfield Proctor turn back the tide of history?"

Frank had always loved history: stories of great men, wars, civilizations, the rise and fall of empires. At Amherst, like many of his classmates, he read Charles Darwin's 1859 essay, *The Origin of Species*. The book had caused a sensation all across Europe and in America. Frank was a devout Christian, and Darwin's revolutionary theories did not threaten his beliefs. But they did seem to explain a lot about the world he was witnessing: natural selection, survival of the fittest. It really did seem to explain the rise of incredibly wealthy and powerful men: railroad barons, steel lords, newspaper titans, banking kings, marble emperors. Everywhere Frank looked, he saw enormously wealthy, extraordinarily powerful and ruthless men growing ever richer and more powerful. Compared to the poor, ignorant laborers they employed for next to nothing, these men really were fitter, naturally singled out by birth and upbringing to succeed.

"It's not hard to make money these days," Proctor told him. "Labor is cheap and plentiful. For every job, there are ten men lined up to choose from."

Frank was on the train to Boston. It was his first solo trip for the company to the Boston office. By 1886, with annual sales of well over $1 million, the Vermont Marble Company had branch offices in half a dozen major U.S. cities. Boston was not the biggest yard, but it was one of the most competitive. All of the major domestic marble producers had offices there or agents. Proctor journeyed there as often as twice a month, where he found the hustle of the rapidly expanding hub bracing and could keep better tabs on the marble industry than he could in Vermont. But with Proctor called to the West Coast to negotiate several deals there, he sent Frank to Boston in his stead.

The company's offices were on the fifth floor of a narrow brick building on Water Street near the harbor. Frank climbed the five stories slowly, skirting boxes and other debris left on the stairs. On one of the landings, a rat scurried out of the way. At the top, a wooden door with a sign, "John C. Allen, Vermont Marble Company," greeted him. He knocked on the door.

"Come in," called a voice on the other side.

Frank opened the door. He was shocked at the chaos that greeted him. He was a fastidious young man, neat almost to compulsion. The small room in front of him looked as if it had just been ransacked. Except for the chair Allen sat in, there was not an empty seat or space in the place. Drawers were pulled out, folders and papers strewn about, boxes and books scattered around the floor. Under the window in back of the large oak desk where Frank could just barely see Allen behind stacks of papers and books, a half dozen sample cases of marble lay open, their contents spilling across the floor.

"You must be Frank," Allen said, rising.

He was a handsome, earnest young man. He stuck his pencil behind his ear and crossed the room to shake hands with Frank.

"Sorry about the mess," Allen said, clearing off a chair for Frank. "It's been a wild few weeks."

Allen was one of those bright young men Proctor was quick to recognize and reward. In two years, Allen had risen from sales agent to stock supervisor to branch manager. In addition to his other duties, Allen was responsible for hiring many of the immigrant laborers who arrived filthy and babbling by the thousands every month at the city's teeming harbor.

The two men talked nonstop as they walked hurriedly to the waterfront to inspect a new shipment of prospective workers. The streets were crowded, and they had to pick their way carefully around carts, people and dog and other animal droppings. At one corner, outside a tavern, a crowd was gathered around two drunkards who were arguing and waving their fists. Frank and Allen stepped into the street to avoid the scene and were nearly run over by a large pushcart.

"Hey, get outta the way!" yelled the cart's owner. "What, d'ya think you own the street?"

At the water's edge, there was more chaos. Frank could hardly process what he saw: Hundreds of poor, dirty, many half-starved, men, women and children stumbling off leaky tubs, blinking at the New World that greeted them. Many carried nothing but the clothes on their backs.

"Do they get any food on the boats?" Frank asked Allen, incredulous at the sight before him. "Some of these people look like they haven't had a decent meal in weeks."

"Not much," Allen replied. "Maybe a cup of watery soup or porridge and a crust of bread a couple of times a day. They herd 'em together like cattle. They barely have space in the hold to lie down to sleep."

"Some of these tubs don't even look seaworthy," Frank said, squinting at the flotilla of bobbing boats.

"Some of them aren't," Allen said. "I've heard of several sinking on the way over. It can be a rough crossing."

"How long does it take?"

"In good weather it should take about twelve days," Allen replied. "If the weather's bad, who knows?" His voice trailed off.

"Most of the captains charge seven dollars a person, and a lot of these people can't even afford that price," Allen continued. "I've had to cover the fare for some of these men. They tell me they have a brother or an uncle who's a good stone cutter and will work off the fare. I've spotted a few of 'em the passage fare."

Frank shook his head. "Already in debt to us before they even get here."

Yes, it really was survival of the fittest, Frank thought as he watched Allen inspect a new prospect, squeezing his arms, looking in his mouth at his teeth and gums.

Frank had recently read a newspaper article that said more than nine million men, women and children had come to America between 1846 and 1875, "and the tide is continuing unabated," the article continued.

"Every year, an average of more than 200,000 people land on our shores, looking for work, a new beginning, a new life," the article went on. "The flow of immigrants is changing the ideal of America as a religious and political haven to America as an economic opportunity. In the process, they are changing the social and cultural fabric of the country."

And also the political fabric, Frank thought. Those men are not just cheap laborers, they are also cheap votes. Plentiful votes. Ignorant votes. It would not take much to organize them.

This fact was brought rudely home to Redfield Proctor in 1884, two years before the great division battle. That year, during the Vermont statewide fall election campaign, one of the Democratic Party's more eloquent standard bearers held a rally in Proctor. (By the 1880s, Redfield Proctor's influence over the village of Sutherland Falls was so complete that people stopped referring to the town as Sutherland Falls and instead called it "Proctor." It is easy to see how the transformation evolved. For the hundreds of newly arrived immigrants who worked in the marble mills and quarries on the banks of Sutherland Falls, most of whom could not read, write or speak English and had never heard of Peter Southerland, "Proctor" was their only connection to their new world, the only English word, concept and reality they knew or needed to know. They did not work for the Vermont Marble Company, they worked for Proctor. They did not live in Sutherland Falls, they lived in Proctor's town. Anything associated with the man was the man, and everything in the workers' lives was associated with Proctor: home, job, church, school, food, sickness, health, birth, death, burial. There was nothing in the workers' lives, or their deaths, that Proctor did not touch. Sutherland Falls had become a company town in name, in fact, and in the most autocratic, patronizing sense of the word. All that was left was the legalities of the name change and division would accomplish that and create a sister village in West Rutland, for good measure.)

When the Democratic challenger came to Proctor in the fall of 1884, he found a large but exceedingly timid natural constituency. It was lunchtime and about one hundred of the men were sitting around a lumber pile near the entrance to one of the mills. It was unusually warm for October, and many of the men had stripped off their outer shirts. They spoke quietly among themselves, a few of them pitched pennies in a sun-splashed corner of the yard. Nearby, another group played cards. Few noticed when the stranger climbed atop one of the lumber piles and began speaking. As he slowly warmed up, however, more and more of the men looked up. Soon, even the men playing cards had ceased their game and were listening intently to the speaker.

Just then Proctor appeared at the far end of the lumber yard, about one hundred yards away. His head was down and he was whittling on a piece of wood, apparently lost in thought. He walked slowly across the yard, outwardly oblivious to the men and activity at the other end of the yard.

At the sight of Proctor, one or two of the workers shifted uneasily. They looked from one to the other. Several of them began slowly edging away from the group. They slipped behind a pile of lumber. Others followed. Soon the yard was quite empty except for the candidate, still balanced precariously on his perch. Sure that he still had the ears of his audience, if not their bodies in front of him, the speaker simply elevated his voice and continued his speech. Proctor disappeared into one of the nearby barns.

That evening Proctor was grim. "We must not let the Democrats come in and organize the workers," he told Frank and Fletcher, his voice determined as he told them how the men had hid from him but continued to listen to the Democratic orator.

"These workers may be poor and ignorant, but they are numerous," Proctor continued. "And they are dangerous precisely because of their ignorance and their numbers."

It was typical of Proctor that he would often speak as eloquently in private as he did in public. He loved the sound of his own voice, the rolling cadences, the mellifluous baritone rising and falling with the emotion of his argument. He did not need a large audience to be eloquent, just his own ear.

"The only way to handle these men is to keep them inferior, to segregate them," Proctor told the boys. "The mistake we are making is to discourage them from continuing their own traditions and ways. Let them worship in their Catholic churches, dress in their own costumes, keep their holidays and celebrations, eat their native dishes and foods. We should not encourage them to learn English. We should stop teaching them to read and write

English. In this way they are doomed to inferiority. If we encourage them to assimilate and emulate, they will only wind up seizing our ways, our ballot boxes and our progress. We must not let them use our own weapons to overtake us. We must keep them victims, otherwise they will become the victors. And that's exactly what will happen if we let the opposition come in and organize them."

Not long after the fall election campaign and the incident in the lumber yard, the unwritten rules of behavior in the community were again challenged. But unlike the first incident, this latest affront was not only openly initiated, it was openly climaxed with no loss of nerve or the convenient anonymity of a lumber pile. There was an open hostility this time, a proud defiance and solidarity that Proctor had never seen or felt among the men before, and it sobered him. So inextricably was he involved and identified with the village and the company and the lives of his workers that every affront, every defiance of authority, had personal overtones. He knew this and knew that the workers knew it, too. It was not just a challenge to the unwritten laws of the community; it was a personal contest. The fact that the challenge was not successful was small consolation to Proctor. The triumph, he knew, was won at the expense of the act itself: the act of independent thought and group identification.

Like all of the citizen boards, social groups, businesses, schools, churches, post office, livery and lodges established ostensibly for the workers in the village of Proctor, the company actually controlled the village school board, not with strong-armed indifference or ruthlessness but quietly with an unassuming if cold dispassion that hid behind clerical collars and grocers' aprons hand picked by Proctor. In fact and in essence, Proctor had filled every chair on the board, although the company's only directly allotted representative was twenty-six-year-old Frank Partridge, the newly appointed assistant treasurer of the Vermont Marble Company.

Even the workers' representative to the board—a small gesture to the ideals of democracy designed to appease the workers—was a company man in disguise. The company dragged him out of his meaningless drudgery with promises of a bigger and better house, meat three times a week for his family and a foreman's job at the mill. There were half a dozen such dragged-out loyalists among the workers who held superficially authoritarian and elected positions in the community. The company called them the "spokesmen" for the workers' concerns. The workers called them company "rats."

They were everywhere, carefully noting actions and words, no matter how trivial, that the company superintendants might find interesting. They were everywhere—except, for the first time, on the school board.

In the last election, the company-backed candidate had been narrowly defeated, an unprecedented result.

Josef Sundqvist, who had arrived in Proctor from Sweden with his wife and two small children only about a year earlier, had narrowly defeated the company candidate in a normally uncontested election and was scheduled to take his seat on the board at that night's meeting.

Nobody knew much about Sundqvist, except that it took him only about three weeks to be tagged as a "trouble maker" by his foreman for helping to save a man trapped under a quarter-ton slab of marble after the foreman had screamed to Sundqvist and the other men in the quarry to get back to work. Ignoring the foreman, Sundqvist, a huge, six-foot-six giant with tremendous arms and chest, lifted one corner of the rough-edged, quarter-ton slab himself as another worker dragged the trapped man, screaming in pain, from under the block.

The story spread quickly through the quarries and mills. Strength, religious faith and family fidelity were perhaps most prized and admired among the immigrants. Almost immediately, Sundqvist became something of a folk hero.

Sundqvist could also speak and write English, which added to his stature among the workers and to his troubles with the foremen. There was a lot of ethnic pride and posturing among the various nationalities living and working in Proctor, but the Swedes, with more than two hundred families in the village, were the largest and dominant clan. From the day of the quarry accident, Sundqvist became the spiritual and—by his very size and strength—the physical leader of the Swedish community. He listened and commiserated with the workers' problems, articulating their concerns to the foremen and teaching a few of them to read English. In little more than a year, Sundqvist had created some powerful enemies.

The first school board meeting after Sundqvist's election had barely been gaveled to order when Frank stood up.

"Mr. Chairman, it has come to my attention that the board's newest member," Frank pursed his lips and glanced at the papers in his hands, "Mr. Josef Sundqvist, has a criminal record in Sweden. He left that country a fugitive. According to the warrant I have in my hand, he is a thief who stole thirty-five dollars from his employer."

A ripple of shock ran through the audience.

Frank continued: "As an accused criminal, Mr. Sundqvist is ineligible to hold any office in this country. It is the unanimous decision of the other board members that he be prohibited from being seated on the board and that new elections be held so that the workers may elect a new representative."

"That is a lie!"

Sundqvist jumped up and glared at Frank.

"That money was owed to me by my employer. He refused to pay me because he knew I wanted it for passage for my family to America. That money was mine. I took no more than what was owed to me—sixteen dollars."

"Mr. Chairman, I have in my hand a letter from Josef Sundqvist's previous employer in Sweden. He states that Mr. Sundqvist stole money from him. He has requested that we attach his pay until the money, plus interest—a total of thirty-five dollars—is paid back to him. Because Mr. Sundqvist has a wife and children to support, we have agreed that this is a fair solution rather than jailing him or firing him. However, he cannot be permitted to sit on this board or hold any public office or any other position within the marble company, his church or any other organization in this community. He is also prohibited from voting in any local or company elections."

"Never!" Sundqvist shouted. "I never stole money. It is a lie."

Sundqvist stood shaking his head furiously.

"That money was mine, and my employer would not pay me because he knew I wanted to leave him to come to America."

"He is an admitted thief," Frank replied, addressing the chairman. "I move that his election be invalidated immediately and new elections scheduled."

Frank sat down.

It was a curious, unlikely moment for a stand. Maybe it was the charge. Nearly all of the workers had run away from something in the old country: sickness, debt, no work, too much work, greedy bosses who cheated them and abused them—the unfairness of it all. All of them had experienced it. A voice vote on Frank's resolution to invalidate Sundqvist's election was roundly defeated.

Panicky, Frank jumped to his feet. Unless something happened quickly, Sundqvist would be seated.

"I move this meeting be adjourned," he said.

The motion was quickly seconded by one of the other board members, a superintendant for the company, who also asked that the vote on adjournment not be a voice vote but a stand up vote. Those in favor of adjournment were to go to one side of the room where they would stand to be counted. Those opposed were to go to the other side of the room.

Frank nodded to the superintendent, relieved.

Perfect, Frank thought. *If the men wanted to defy their superiors, they would have to stand up and be counted. No hiding in the anonymity of a voice vote.*

A hush fell over the room as the vote procedure was explained. The men looked from one to another, unsure what to do. An air of frustration, defeat, despair hung over them. For several minutes no one moved, then slowly, Sundqvist stood up, drawing himself to his full six feet, six inches. He turned and walked slowly and deliberately, his steps echoing in the silent room, to the side designated "opposed."

Sundqvist stood alone, defiantly. There was a scraping of chairs and feet as the rest of the men stood up and began to divide themselves. Hesitantly, with bowed heads, many of the workers began to join Sundqvist, huddling together in a tight band.

Frank whispered to two of the superintendants near him. They nodded and began to wave their arms in the air to the company loyalists on the side of the room that favored adjournment. The men understood and began to mill back and forth across the room so that an accurate count was impossible.

"The motion to adjourn is still before the board," the harried chairman announced.

The superintendant who had seconded Frank's original call to adjourn, then asked for a signed, paper vote. Those who favored adjournment would use a blue ballot; those opposed, yellow.

At last, the workers had been divided and conquered. Each had to sign his name on a single, solitary strip of paper for all to see today, tomorrow and the day after that, every day for the rest of their lives in this community. There was no strength in numbers now, no group, no six-foot, six-inch giant hovering over them. Just one man, one piece of paper.

The blues won the day, unanimously since the yellows all abstained rather than attach their names to their defiance. The meeting adjourned.

No new election to replace Sundqvist on the school board was ever held. But it was a hollow, meaningless victory for his supporters since the board never met again.

These were small incidents, but to Redfield Proctor, they held enormous significance. Instinctively, he knew these men, however ignorant, represented a huge threat to the established order, to *his* established order. In fact, their very ignorance, combined with their sheer numbers, was their most dangerous attribute. Their ignorance led them to believe their eyes, and their eyes told them that Proctor paid too little attention to their miseries. At the same time, their simple logic suggested to them that since they formed the bulk of the people in their little world, their miseries should count for something. It would not take a whole lot of eloquence to win their votes, just a little attention and a few promises. The sudden ascendency to power of a little-known Democrat named William Hogan proved that.

At that time, every town in the state, no matter its size, had one representative to the Vermont House of Representatives. In past election years, the town of Rutland could be counted on as a firm rock bed of Republican support by a wide margin. But the growing influx of laboring men brought in by Proctor to work his marble quarries and run his marble mills was beginning to change the political landscape of the town. If properly organized, the struggling Democratic Party could score big in Rutland in upcoming elections. Hogan's election to the Vermont state legislature in 1884—the first Democrat ever elected from Rutland to the state legislature—had proved that.

With the presidential election of 1888 now a little more than two years away, Proctor knew he had to act quickly to stem the tide of revolt. The mistake Hogan and the Democrats made was not to take themselves as seriously as Proctor did.

"From the fact that the laboring men have elected a representative by such an overwhelming vote, the Republicans seem to infer that the town is in a state of anarchy down there," Hogan laughed to other members of the House after Proctor submitted his petition to the chamber to divide Rutland.

"Is my presence so threatening?" Hogan continued. "Is my election proof that the voters of Rutland are turbulent?"

Hogan seemed genuinely flattered that a man of his little stature could garner the attention of the most powerful man in his district and a former governor. The great public outcry against Proctor and division only inflated Hogan's ego further.

"What is Governor Proctor so afraid of?" Hogan asked. "Certainly, he can't be afraid of someone as inconsequential as myself or a few poor working men. How does my election prove the voters are so out of control or so dangerous that we must divide them up into small detachments?"

In 1886, Hogan and the Democrats proved they were a party better off not in power. Once achieved, they did not seem to know what to do with power or how to keep it. They seemed better suited and more effective in the role of outsider than insider, rabble rouser than rabble leader.

"Hogan, in his mistaken view of himself, thinks his support is widespread in the town," Proctor told Frank and Fletcher dismissively.

"If he studied the returns, as I do, he would realize that East Rutland, the main business and commercial center of the town, is reliably Republican. Where the opposition has made gains is among the immigrant laborers and poor working men in West Rutland and Proctor. Those new votes have offset our strength in the east."

The symbolism of Hogan's victory was not lost on Proctor. Even though, as a practical matter, Rutland had no more political clout than any other town in the state since every town had just one vote, as the largest town it had great influence. It was also Proctor's home town.

"I cannot abide having the town where I reside be Democratic!" Proctor told the boys. "Or the company I own be considered a Democratic machine. Those men work for me! Not the opposition!"

In 1886, Proctor and the Vermont Marble Company employed more than 1,200 men. Several hundred more laborers also resided in the greater Rutland area, working for other smaller Rutland Town marble mills under the influence, if not the actual ownership, of the VMC. With their fortunes so closely tied to their jobs, employees of the Vermont Marble Company could be counted on to vote as they thought their employer's interests demanded. If they could be divided up—"color-coded," so to speak—by town, as the ballots had been divided and color-coded at the school board meeting, the men, to a man, could be counted on to mark their ballots as they thought their employer would want them to mark them. Or not mark a ballot at all. In this way, Proctor could make Republicans out of voters who under other circumstances would be attracted to another party and, in the process, triple Rutland's power in the state legislature.

Beyond increasing the region's influence on state and national elections and politics, Proctor was also anxious to reestablish the Republican Party at the grass-roots level as well.

"Listers, selectmen, these are the real machinery of government," Proctor explained to Frank and Fletcher.

Proctor disliked the thought that working men, or even worse, black men, should hold any kind of power over their own destiny, let alone his. By birth and by breeding and social status, he considered himself infinitely qualified and destined to be a leader of men. After all, he was fitter, naturally selected out for this role.

Not even so obscure an election as a justice of the peace could escape Proctor's attention.

At that time, all towns in the state over fifteen thousand in population were entitled to a maximum of fifteen justices of the peace. When division was proposed, the West Rutland town charter that accompanied that town's division proposal included a provision that called for having justices of the peace chosen in the last election serve in the town where they were legal voters. This provision was already part of the original Rutland town charter. Thus, in West Rutland and Rutland, only justices who were legal voters of those two towns could serve out their terms following division.

But this clause was ingeniously left out of the Proctor town charter that accompanied that town's division proposal. This meant that once division was accomplished, justices of the peace who resided in Proctor and who had been elected prior to division had no legal status. With no provision for filling these slots, the governor was asked to appoint justices of the peace for the town of Proctor.

This sequence of events had the effect of nullifying the election of George Putnam, a Negro who had been elected a justice of the peace in Proctor in the 1884 election.

Ingenious, indeed.

Chapter 14

MILL

From the back door of Proctor's estate, Frank could just barely make out the figure of Proctor inside the door of one of the mill buildings. It was late afternoon, and the cool shadows were beginning to lengthen, but Proctor was jacketless.

It was about four o'clock, and Frank was surprised to see him. He knew Proctor's meeting with Ripley had been at two in Center Rutland. *Was a short meeting good or bad?* he wondered nervously.

Proctor was in the midst of an animated discussion. Frank could see his right arm pointing to what looked like some papers, or maybe it was a book, in his other hand. Frank could not see who Proctor was talking to but guessed it was probably Sam. Sam Howard had been a classmate of Frank and Fletcher at Amherst. He was from western New York state. Proctor, an instant judge of character, had liked him immediately and quickly "snatched him up," as he so often did whenever he met a young man who impressed him. As with all the young men he gathered around him, Proctor had put Sam in a responsible position. He was head of operations at the mill.

Frank jogged clumsily down the broad sloping lawn of Proctor's estate, across the railroad tracks and through the huge double doors of the wooden mill building. The ear-splitting whine of the wire cutters greeted him, bringing him up short. He frowned in pain from the noise, breathing heavily from his exertion.

In front of him, swinging "gangs"—three-sided wooden frames—used a combination of wire, sand, water and friction to rough cut the marble blocks down to size. The top arm of the wooden gang reached back to a steam engine that powered the frame and gave it its swinging motion. Wire bands, which served as the blades of the saw, were stretched tightly from one end of the frame to the other. A mixture of sand and water flowed over the block from above and furnished the teeth for the saw. The water came from the nearby Otter Creek. The sand was carted in by hand in great wheelbarrows by dirty, sweating men, muscles bulging, from a giant sand hill in the yard outside. The crashing Sutherland Falls produced the energy that powered the steam engines that drove the gangs. Some fifteen swinging gangs filled the long wooden mill building along the bank of the creek. Several more wooden mill buildings, even longer than this one, stood beyond.

As soon as a block was sawed down, two men, bent in a crouch, would hurry forward and roll it out from under the gang still swinging on its way back up. Another pair of men would roll a new slab on a low cart into place. Frank watched the men jockey the rough marble into position, inching it this way and that until they had it positioned under the gang exactly where the cutter had marked it to be sawed. The men braced the cart with wooden timbers. One of them motioned with his arm and the gang swung lower.

With a horrific screech, worse than the dying screams of any animal, the wire saw bit into the block, swinging back and forth, its whine rising and rising and rising, unrelenting. A fine mist of sand and water flew out from the stone. Frank saw sparks fly as the white-hot wire slowly cut through the block.

He lowered his head against the noise of the saw. It seemed to take forever to bite its way through the stone. Finally, it reached the bottom and began swinging its way quickly back up through the rock.

Frank felt that he could finally breathe again. He walked over to the foreman rubbing his hand over the edges of the stone, still hot from the friction of the saw.

The foreman inspected the cut carefully, measuring the block with his pocket tape. Satisfied, he nodded to the men.

"Move it over to the rubbing bed," he barked. "Let's go, let's go. We don't have all day."

"Where's this block going?" Frank asked, coming up to inspect the work of the cutters himself.

"This one'll go right to the finishing shop, sir," the foreman said, standing up to face Frank. "We could run the gangs all night long and still not catch up with the backlog on Extra White. Look at that," he said, brushing his hand down the face of the block. "Did ya ever see such an even vein? Not a flaw in it."

Frank watched the men as they rolled the rough-edged block next door to the rubbing beds where it would be squared and worked down by hand to its exact size and all the scratches and burrs and scars removed. After using small hammers and chisels to smooth out the roughest spots, planers with thick splayed fingers would spread wet sand over all the exposed faces of the stone and rub the sand over and over and over by hand with small blocks of metal until the sides were as smooth as silk. From there, the block would go to the polishers who would rub it some more before finally sending it to the loading dock where it would be crated and readied for transport.

Out of the corner of his eye, Frank saw Proctor motion to him, and he went over to join him. As he had thought, Proctor was with Sam Howard. He guessed they were discussing the order for the new court building in Washington, D.C. Frank knew the job was badly behind schedule. There had been several accidents at the quarries in recent weeks. One of the quarrymen had gotten drunk (drinking on the job was becoming a real problem among some of the men), slipped and fallen nearly eighty feet to his death. Two others had had limbs crushed in separate accidents. Yesterday, four more of the gangs had broken down, bringing to twelve—out of seventy-four here at the falls—the number of gangs out of commission. It would take at least several more days to repair them.

As Howard looked up to greet him, Frank could see the worry on his face. He gave him what he hoped was a smile of encouragement.

"Frank, my boy, just in time to hear the good news," Proctor said jovially.

Frank was taken aback. *Good news?* he thought. The court building was behind schedule, twelve gangs were down, the division struggle was a mess and Proctor's meeting with Ripley was already over. How could there be good news?

He tried to discern if Proctor's conviviality was really some kind of black humor but saw his pleasure was genuine. Frank allowed himself to relax—a little.

"I was just telling Sam that we've landed the contract for the new Arlington Memorial in Washington. It'll be the largest cemetery monument in the world."

"Wheeew!" Frank whistled under his breath. *No wonder Howard looked worried!*

"Sam and I were just discussing expanding the hours at the mill," Proctor continued. "Right now, the men are working ten and one-half hours a day. I think we need to go to twelve-hour days. What do you think, Frank?"

"What about the equipment?" Frank asked. "We've got at least a dozen of our gangs down."

Sam broke in. "We're working on that. We should have all of them back up in a day or two at the most. Right now, the bottleneck is in the mill. I don't think we need to expand the hours for the other operations, at least not yet. Not until we catch up here."

"Good." Proctor nodded in agreement. "We'll go with twelve-hour shifts here until we clear this backlog and get the gangs back up and then bump the other operations up. What would you say, another week?"

"Hmmm, it depends on how fast we can bring these gangs back online," Howard said, thinking. "Maybe five days."

"What happened on that new cathedral in St. Louis?" Frank asked. "Are we getting that job?"

Proctor laughed. "Renwick, the cathedral architect, let it be known that if I would offer him the option of taking three thousand shares of stock any time within the next two years at thirty dollars a share, it might induce him to favor us in that contract."

"Are you serious?" Howard asked.

"Is Renwick serious?" Frank asked.

"He was perfectly serious," Proctor replied. "The man's out of his head. We have the low bid locked up. Thompson gave us the other bids in advance. Renwick's either a greedy fool, stupid or both. I told him if he didn't resign the commission immediately and never work in marble again, I just might be induced to favor him with a blackball that would guarantee he'd never get another commission in marble or any other material, for that matter."

Frank and Howard chuckled.

"What'd he say," Howard asked.

"Last I heard he was thinking of giving up working in marble," Proctor said. "Too 'ostentatious,' he says. By the way, that reminds me. Now that I've got you two boys here, I need your opinion on another matter. What do you think about expanding our list to include the mud layer and glass that are too poor to go for common stock?"

"You mean add a lower grade?" Frank asked, looking dubiously at Howard.

"Exactly," Proctor replied. "Could you sell quite a quantity if the price was low enough?"

"Well, yeah," Howard said. "I would think we could sell it for building stock that doesn't show. Right now, common is really too good for that."

"What would the price need to be at the quarry?" Proctor asked.

"It would need to be cheap," Frank replied. "Our margins on common stock are not all that high. And we would have to sell this grade cheaper than that."

"That's true, but right now it's just going for waste," Howard said. "So it's actually costing us money. I wager we could quarry it out for pretty damn near the same price we're hauling it out as waste now."

The three men stood talking a few minutes longer before Sam, catching sight of two of his lieutenants, bid Proctor and Frank farewell and hurried off.

Proctor and Frank walked outside into the low, slanting sun, lowering their voices as they left the din of the mill behind. The peak foliage had passed, and the ground was littered with dead leaves. A mild breeze swirled around the yard. Indian summer was Frank's favorite season. He felt the warmth of the setting sun on his face. Too soon, he knew, winter would be here.

On the tracks next to them, flatbed cars loaded with jagged rough blocks of marble from the quarries in West Rutland, one and sometimes two to a car, rolled steadily by on their way to the mill. One of Proctor's first actions at the very beginning of his political career as a first-term state representative from Rutland in 1868 had been to propose an amendment to a bill authorizing the Bennington & Rutland Railroad to extend its railroad to West Rutland. Under Proctor's amendment, the railroad would not be able to charge any more than fifty cents a ton for hauling marble. The fruits of that amendment rolled by Frank and Proctor now as they walked across the yard back up to Proctor's house. Transportation may have been one of the key elements in the marble business, but at a cost of fifty cents a ton, it had also proven to be one of the cheapest elements for Proctor to solve.

"How did your meeting with Ripley go," Frank asked. "Did you have to offer to buy his company?"

"Yes," Proctor replied, looking away.

"So, he's going to testify for us?"

Proctor did not say anything for a few moments. He turned back to Frank and smiled ruefully. "Yes, he is. He's actually looking forward to it."

"I nearly forgot," Frank said. "Mrs. Myers sent William, her caretaker, to ask if you could meet her in your office this evening."

"Did she say what about?"

"Something about Smedburg. Apparently, he's raising a fuss about some stock purchases you made recently."

"God, how that man provokes me!" Proctor said annoyed. "I make a few trades, and *he* gets upset. He knows absolutely nothing about the marble business! He goes around with this very exaggerated idea of the value of his stock. He doesn't realize the business is not the same as it was after the war. We shall never see profits like that again. Lord, how his conduct provokes me!"

He walked on, fuming. It was unlike Proctor to carry on like this. He had an exceedingly calm demeanor. He was unflappable, maintaining an imperturbable equanimity that often exasperated his opponents. Nothing, it seemed, could provoke him. Frank could not recall ever seeing Proctor angry or rarely even upset. He got over setbacks and disputes quickly and never carried a grudge. There were very few men he truly disliked. Dorr was one, although Proctor considered him more a political foe, or opponent, than a real enemy. Proctor was a true man of the people. Enemies were rare, although lately Frank had noticed that the mere mention of Adolphus Smedburg's name could rouse in Proctor an impatience he had never seen before.

"I never should have let him into the company," Proctor continued. "He is vicious and mean, and the only way to deal with him is to get rid of him."

He turned to Frank. "That is one fight I am truly going to relish."

They had reached the house.

"I told William to bring Mary 'round in about an hour," Frank said. "Should I ask him to have Mrs. Myers meet you another time?"

"No, no. I can see her tonight. Ask her to meet me at six in Center Rutland. Fletcher and Dillingham are due back from Montpelier around eight, so that will give us a couple of hours to discuss Mr. Smedburg."

"Fletcher went to Montpelier?" Frank asked, surprised.

"Yes. I had him accompany Dillingham to meet with some of our people in Montpelier to gauge our support on the division question. They should be back around eight to give us a report of what the members are thinking."

Frank said nothing, lowering his head to hide the glow of triumph he felt. So Proctor knew after all that Fletcher had come into the office this morning hung over! That Frank's excuse about Fletcher missing his morning meeting with his father because he was tied up at the mill was a lie.

A couple of times during the day Frank had wondered about Fletcher and where he was. But the day had been so busy that Frank had quickly forgotten him, not really caring anyway.

So, Fletcher was in Montpelier, Frank thought. *Fletcher detests Montpelier! And hung over!* Frank smiled to himself, thinking of Fletcher bouncing and rattling on the train to the state capital, hung over.

Frank turned away from Proctor's gaze to hide his pleasure. He knew that sending Fletcher off to Montpelier had been Proctor's form of punishment, his way of letting his son—and Frank—know that he knew exactly what was going on.

Frank could hardly contain himself as he thought of Fletcher's misery, hung over, dragged around the capital. And himself, vindicated.

Chapter 15

PLAN

Frank drove Proctor back to Center Rutland in Redfield's carriage. By the time they arrived it was after five, and the sun was almost straight in their faces as it began its dip below the mountains. The shadows were long, and the breeze, warm and playful that afternoon, had turned chilly in the lengthening shadows. There would surely be a frost that night.

The men hadn't eaten. Nothing, in fact, had been said about dinner. Ever since Fannie had died three years before, Proctor had become almost obsessive about the dinner hour. Whenever he was at home, he insisted that all the family must be together for dinner. Out of town was the only excuse he tolerated for missing the family dinner. Even Arabella and Fletcher, who were both married with their own houses, were often there, as was Emily, seventeen, and Redfield Jr., seven, both still at home. Like all the Proctor get-togethers, it was a noisy, boisterous affair, Proctor dominating but encouraging his children to talk, discuss school, happenings in the community and, of course, politics. His children not only had to talk, they had to have an opinion. He insisted on it. There were almost always guests for dinner, mostly business and political allies of Proctor, sometimes school chums of the children, and they joined in the banter and discussions. No matter what had happened during the day or how busy he was, Proctor always reserved the dinner hour for his children. This was the first evening Frank could remember Proctor being in town and missing supper.

The thought of food made Frank's already churning stomach do another somersault. He glanced at his timepiece in the sinking light as they pulled into the driveway leading to Proctor's office—5:20. The Fortnightly Society held its meetings downtown at the Opera House. The meetings were supposed to begin at 6:30 p.m., but it was always closer to 6:50 or 7:00 before the informal greetings and chitchat quieted down, and people took their seats. Tonight's meeting would likely take even longer to settle down what with Julia's guest, Louisa May Alcott, there.

Frank felt his breast pocket again for about the tenth time that day. His poem was still there. If the meeting started at 7:00, worst case—*God, I hope it starts at 7:00,* Frank thought—he would just barely have time to say a few words of welcome to Miss Alcott, read his poem and leave by 7:30 to get back here at 8:00 to meet Fletcher and Dillingham. *Please let everyone be early,* he prayed. He hoped Miss Alcott would not be offended by his hasty departure. He hoped Julia would understand. She had been counting on him to host the evening. Frank glanced at his timepiece again. *Of all nights!* he thought miserably. *Why did the Fortnightly Society meeting have to be tonight?*

Mary Myers was waiting for them when Proctor and Frank arrived. One of the young office clerks had let her into Proctor's office, and she sat there now in one of the chairs near the fire, which was burning brightly. She got up to greet them.

"Hello, Frank," she said, extending her hand and smiling at him. "It's so good to see you. I understand that Louisa May Alcott is coming to Rutland for a reading tomorrow evening."

"Yes, she's giving a public reading at the library," Frank said. "The Fortnightly Society is holding a little private welcoming for her this evening."

"Don't forget Fletcher and Dillingham will be here at eight," Proctor interrupted.

"I haven't forgotten, sir," Frank said. The knot in his stomach tightened.

"I'm just going to run by and pay my respects. I promised…" he caught himself just as he was about to say, "Julia," and stammered, "the others. I promised the others I would come by for a few minutes."

"Are there still any seats left for Miss Alcott's reading tomorrow?" Mary asked.

"I don't think so. But I'm sure I could arrange for you to come. Would you like me to reserve a seat for you?"

"Would you? That would be ever so lovely of you. I'm sure John's twenty-eight-year-old daughter, Nellie, would like to go as well. We were speaking about it this afternoon. Now you better run along, Frank. If you have to be back by eight, that doesn't give you much time."

She came over and straightened Frank's collar. "I'm sure your poem will be a big hit," she told him quietly, brushing his jacket and squeezing both his arms.

Startled, Frank smiled in gratitude, feeling a glow of warmth spread over him at her touch. Mary released him. His arms were still warm where she had held him.

"Now, get going," she told him.

"Thank you," he said, turning to leave. "I'll be sure to put those tickets aside for you and Miss Nellie."

As Frank left them, Mary turned to Proctor and smiled. "Hello Governor. Thank you for seeing me on such short notice."

"Not at all."

He came over and took her hand. "Thank you for coming out at this hour."

He escorted her back to her chair and helped her sit.

"Frank and I have a meeting later this evening with Dillingham and Fletcher anyhow, so this is perfectly convenient. Can I get you something?"

"Yes, tea would be nice."

"I'll tell John, the clerk."

Proctor got up and went to the door. "John," he called. "Would you get Mrs. Myers and myself some tea? And see if you can rustle up some bread and cheese and some jam as well."

Proctor closed the door and came back, taking the chair across from Mary.

"My dear, to what do I owe the pleasure of your company?" He gazed at her fondly.

"Are you quite sure you don't want me to go to Washington with you?" Mary asked coyly.

"It's not that I don't want you to go, my dear," Proctor said, inhaling deeply. "Emily's insisting on accompanying me."

"Tell her she'll be bored. You'll be in meetings all day. Tell her the journey is too long."

"I've told her all that. But she's taken it into her head that she wants to go. She says she'll shop while I'm in meetings. She says the journey is not long, and besides, she worries about me going about alone so much."

"She doesn't suspect anything, does she?" Mary asked anxiously.

"Heavens, no," Proctor replied. "She is just having one of her whims—that's all. She's bored here and has it in her head that she needs a new wardrobe and a shopping expedition to Washington is just the cure."

He sighed. "Well, we'd better get down to business. We don't have much time. I understand Mr. Smedburg has been to see you. What does our esteemed treasurer want this time?"

"He *wanted* to come see me, but I told him no," Mary corrected him. "So he sent me a lengthy wire instead."

Proctor laughed. "Not exactly a love letter, I'm sure."

"Not exactly," she replied.

"What's his complaint?"

"The usual. The stock, expenses. He says expenses are too high, the stock price is too low, and that you made some very large purchases of stock without notifying him ahead of time."

"Is that all?" Proctor asked.

Just then, John, the young clerk, knocked softly on the door and entered with a tray of steaming tea and hot cider, and a plate of cakes, bread and jam and cut up apples and cheese.

"The next time I'm in a meeting with someone, wait to enter the room until I tell you to come in," Proctor told him sharply.

The boy blanched. "Yes sir. I—I—I'm sorry," he stammered.

"Don't let it happen again," Proctor replied.

The young clerk poured the tea for them, his hands shaking and the tea cups rattling. Proctor watched him coldly. The boy passed the tray to each of them.

"Thank you, John," Mrs. Myers said kindly.

The boy offered it to Proctor.

"Just leave it on the table," he said.

"Yes, sir."

John put the tray down. "Is there anything else, sir?" he asked Proctor.

"No, that will be all. Thank you," Proctor said. "I'm expecting Fletcher and Mr. Dillingham a little later. Please be sure the lamp is lit."

"Yes, sir."

"You may leave as soon as Frank returns."

"Yes, sir."

The boy closed the door quietly behind him.

"How that man provokes me!" Proctor said when John had left them alone again.

"Who?" Mary asked, startled.

"Smedburg. He persistently states what is not correct in regard to the business and profits of the company. He uses his best efforts to prevent anybody selling shares at a reasonable price, and puts himself at nearly every opportunity in a hostile attitude, unnecessarily and foolishly so. He really knows nothing about marble and is of no practical value to the company except to make the occasional transfers of shares of stock. The treasurer's work is practically all done here by Frank, and the formal reports might be made here as well with no addition of expense. I have been extremely patient and long suffering, but when this division fight is over, I am determined to end this matter and break his power in the company once and for all."

"He is an awful man," Mary agreed. "He always has been. His little weasel ways and shriveled up body make me uncomfortable."

She shuddered. Proctor smiled at her. His irritation softened at her words and shudder.

"He is the meanest and most vicious man I have ever met," Proctor went on. "He never makes any allowance for depreciation or exhaustion of the property. In fact, a great deal must be done constantly to keep up the property at present value, but he has no grasp of this. In the good years of '81, '82 and '83, we quarried an enormous amount of marble from the very best part of our quarries at West Rutland and here, and where it was the easiest to get. We shall never see another time at either place where we can produce so large an amount of good marble so cheaply."

"But can you really break his power?" Mary asked. "The New York interest is very strong."

"Yes, but don't forget, I control this company. They will come 'round. Once they know what Smedburg is doing to the value of the shares of stock, they'll come over to us."

"What were the stock purchases you made that upset him so dreadfully?" Mary asked, gazing evenly at Proctor, no coyishness, no guile. She was all business.

"I am buying stock to give to the boys, Frank, Sam Howard, John Allen and some of the other young men we have," Proctor said. "They are exceptionally fine young men. I have been training them up ever since I first commenced business, and it is the best point I have ever made. There cannot be selected the world over in the marble business twenty men so capable as we have in our service. If they had an interest in the stock, they would be bound to us for life. Of course, I cannot part with my controlling interest, and I have but little more. That's why I made those purchases. I am anxious to have the boys get as much interest as possible in the company and so attach them permanently to our business."

Mary nodded. "Yes, they are fine young men."

"The whole course of the marble business has so changed that Smedburg is entirely unfamiliar with it," Proctor went on.

"Well, certainly the course of profits has changed," Mary replied. "I think Mr. Smedburg continues to judge it the way it was for a short time after the war. But it is changing constantly in the direction of reduced profits."

"Exactly right!" Proctor nodded in agreement. "We are doing every possible thing in the way of reducing expenses. We made a general reduction of 15 percent last month, and we will make another reduction soon—taking everything, my own salary and all of the help, except the lowest priced laborers who get $1.15 a day."

There was a knock on the door.

"Yes, come," Proctor called.

Frank stuck his head in the door.

"Heavens! Is it eight o'clock already?" Mary exclaimed, jumping up. Proctor also rose.

"Nearly," Frank said. "The train from Montpelier just pulled in. I heard the whistle as I was coming in the drive. Fletcher and Dillingham should be on their way."

"Thank you," Proctor said as Frank withdrew.

Proctor went over to Mary and embraced her quickly.

"I'm going to miss you," Mary whispered. They kissed.

"I almost forgot," Proctor said, pulling away. "I have a surprise for you,"

"You're going to leave Emily home after all?"

He laughed. "No, but while I'm in Washington, I'm going to take a house for the winter."

"You are? A house? For the winter?"

"Yes. A great deal of our work is in Washington. I need to go there often. If I take a house it will give me," he smiled at her, "and you, a place to meet. Staying at your house there would cause too much talk."

"Redfield, that's a wonderful idea!"

They kissed again. Proctor pulled away quickly. "As much as I hate it to be so, you must be on your way. Fletcher and Dillingham will be here any minute."

He escorted her to her carriage. Frank was hard at work at his desk as they passed.

"How was your reception tonight for Miss Alcott?" Mary asked him.

"It went very well," Frank replied. "She's extremely cordial. Very quiet, but a genius. You could tell."

"It's a pity you couldn't have stayed longer," Mary said. "Did she like your poem?"

Frank blushed. "Why yes, yes, I think she did," he finally said. "Of course, she's so polite she would never say she didn't," he added apologetically.

"She wouldn't say it because it isn't true." Mary smiled at him. "Good night, Frank."

"Good night, Mrs. Myers. I'll have those tickets for you and Miss Nellie delivered to the Bardwell tomorrow morning."

"Thank you. That's very thoughtful of you."

"Brrrr, it's getting cold out," Proctor shuddered as he returned from putting Mary in her carriage. He was rubbing his hands together. "Is there any more of that hot cider left?"

He and Frank went into Proctor's office.

"Have you seen the afternoon's *Herald*?" Frank asked.

"Oh no, not another editorial?" Proctor said.

"Yes, this one calls you, 'nothing more than a cheap political boss,' and calls division 'a blatant grab for power.'"

"Do you have it?"

Frank showed Proctor the paper.

"'Division is unjust, uncalled for, and prejudicial to the best interests of all the townspeople with the exception of one individual, Governor Proctor,'" Proctor read the editorial out loud. "'The members of the legislature have taken a solemn oath to protect the interests of all the people of the state, not of one person only. We demand that division be put to a popular vote of the townspeople. If the matter were to be voted on, the legislature would then clearly see that no more than 300 of the 16,000 residents of the town support division, and those 300 have direct ties to Governor Proctor. Division is nothing more than a blatant grab for power by a cheap political boss with delusions of grandeur.'"

Proctor put down the editorial. "Cheap political boss," he muttered. "Delusions of grandeur. Hah! We'll see about that!"

He handed the *Herald* back to Frank, his lips pursed tight.

"That reminds me," he said, his mood suddenly brightening. "Would you get hold of a copy of the *Republican* of yesterday? I understand there's a report in it about your humble servant and his 'grandiose dreams of empire.'

I must confess, the whole scheme is a mystery to me, but I suppose I should acquaint myself with how an empire works, since we are very soon about to be the proud owners of one."

Proctor nodded, amused, at Frank. Frank was unsure if Proctor was kidding or serious, but he scribbled a note to himself to get a copy of yesterday's *Republican* for Proctor. Personally, Frank thought the whole business was going very badly. He could see no way how Proctor could win this one. Everyone was against them. The attacks were ruthless.

"This morning, Robinson over at the feed store told me there was serious talk around town that if division succeeds, the merchants of Rutland will set up a custom house and inaugurate a system of protective tariffs on their goods," Frank told Proctor.

Proctor chuckled. "Then, you know what we shall do, Frank, my boy? We shall retaliate by burning all the bridges between Rutland and the west and the north save one, and charge a toll to anyone coming this way. We will have them, Frank, because West Rutland is the vital link to Albany and the Hudson."

The joke was about to launch Proctor into his favorite pastime of Civil War reminisces and analyses—how foolish the Confederate states had been in not thinking an embargo would be the first response of the industrialized north to any rumblings of secession—when Fletcher and Dillingham stomped in, bringing a rush of cold air with them.

"Brrrr, it's cold out there. It'll snow tonight for sure." William Dillingham swept off his hat and shivered before the fire. He loosened his long wool topcoat and rubbed his hands together.

"And how is everything in our fair capital?" Proctor moved over to Dillingham, and the two men shook hands and greeted each other warmly.

"Fairly reeking," Dillingham replied.

The two men laughed loudly, a joke among intimates over the muddy, backwater outpost that served as the state's capital city.

Dillingham had very high color and his youthful face was flushed bright pink from the cold.

"I have never seen the members so strongly united," Dillingham told Proctor after the four of them were seated before the fire. He sipped a steaming glass of hot cider.

"Hogan is strutting around like some kind of king, he's so puffed up with young Percy Clement's editorials in the *Herald*," Fletcher broke in.

Fletcher's face was still as red as when he first came into the room. Frank knew he had been drinking.

"Yes, I'm afraid, Redfield, this time the members are not going to be shaken," Dillingham said. "Fletcher's right. Clement and all his ranting in the *Herald* have created a huge wave of sympathy for Hogan and the opposition. There was another editorial this afternoon."

"Yes, I saw it," Proctor said.

"Hogan is viewed as some sort of martyr," Dillingham continued. "A Democrat gets elected for the first time in history, and the Proctor machine reacts by not just beating him straight up in the next election but by carving him up into thirds and throwing him back to the people. I tell you, the issue has become almost irrationally emotional. People and members who normally would not know the difference or care to know the difference are joining the cause against us. The issue has transgressed its original premise as a simple move to divide a town that is too large. Somehow, the issue has gotten bigger than that in people's thinking. It has become associated in their minds with every indignity and every injustice they have ever suffered at the hands of outside authority. They could not do anything about that. But here, here is an injustice they can do something about. The issue has become a catchall, Redfield, and you the catchall villain. It's a rap that is unfair. The issue should be decided on the facts and the merits of the case; not on emotion. As a fellow lawyer you know, Redfield, that when emotions are involved, reason and common sense go out the window."

"Are you advising that we withdraw our petition?" Proctor stared at Dillingham.

"I cannot advise you, Redfield, you know that. I can only give you the facts and the situation as straight as I can. And the facts are that the sentiment against you is very strong, stronger than I have ever seen it. The members are aiming to make the proposal, which means you, a convenient symbol. There is the feeling that you have gotten too big, that you need to be cut down to size, and that this is the issue the members appear willing to make a stand on because there is so much widespread popular and prestigious sentiment against it. If truth be told, they are hiding behind the *Herald*. All of Percy Clement's ranting and raving has given them the perfect cover to vote against you. The sentiment on this thing is like a locomotive. It's picking up steam and speed and momentum and everything else in its path. Momentum is very important, Redfield, and right now the momentum is with the opposition."

"I don't want to hear about momentum," Proctor said. "I want to know how many members can we count on?"

Dillingham shook his head. "Truthfully? We have perhaps fifty solid votes. If the vote were taken today, the proposal would go down in flames."

"Are you counseling withdrawal?" Proctor asked again.

Dillingham shook his head again. "I'm not counseling anything. I'm just counting votes."

"Fletcher?" Proctor wanted all of their opinions.

"I say we should proceed," Fletcher replied boastfully. "When it comes to a vote, you'll see. They won't dare oppose us. Right now, it's all talk."

Dillingham pursed his lips and shook his head slightly, frowning.

"Frank?" Proctor asked.

"I think the question is not whether we should withdraw or proceed," Frank said slowly, deliberately. "I think the question we should be discussing is how we are going to succeed. What should be our strategy here? Dillingham has laid out a very bleak picture. And yes, it will be a tough slog. But we have a lot of resources at our disposal. I think we should be discussing strategy, not withdrawal."

Proctor sat back in his chair, a small, satisfied expression on his face as he looked at Frank from under half-closed eyes.

"We all read the papers," Frank continued. "We know our cause is not popular with the people, and Clement is just fanning the flames with all of his inflammatory editorials. As Dillingham says, the sentiment against division in the House appears to be very strongly against us. We are at a critical juncture, but I would advise that a retreat would be more harmful to us in the future than even a defeat. In sum, I think we have no alternative but to stay the course. Our charge now is to plot a course to victory."

Proctor had closed his eyes as Frank spoke, stroking his beard and nodding slowly in agreement. He suddenly sat upright.

"Frank is right," he said. "If we withdraw now, it will only embolden them. We must not let the labor element gain at any level. Listers, justices of the peace, town officials, state representatives. These are the vital cogs of government. They have already succeeded in electing Hogan to the legislature and a Negro, of all things, a justice of the peace. No, the time is ripe for us; we must strike now and not only halt further progress by the opposition, but reverse the gains they have already made. The timing is essential. We have only two years before the next presidential election to organize. We must not withdraw and hand them a victory. At the same time, if we lose we will never recover either. Frank is right, we must not withdraw, and we must not lose. Our only course is to plot a strategy for winning. It has to be overwhelming. Winning against such enormous odds will only increase our stature and power and influence, not only now but for years to come. Yes, gentlemen, we have a great opportunity before us. As Frank says, our task is not to debate whether we should continue or not. This is not the time for timidity. We know we are right. Our task is to turn all of our efforts and all of our energy and resources to attaining victory. It is a huge task. On the surface it looks impossible, but it is the very impossibility of the task that will enable us to win. The opposition is too confident. They think they have the momentum as Dillingham says. They are drunk on Clement. That will make our victory easier, and even sweeter and more impressive when we prevail."

Proctor was standing now, pacing back and forth before the fire.

"This is what I want from each of you."

Proctor was in high gear now. He stood in front of them ticking off commands so rapidly that Frank, who was well-accustomed to Proctor's rapid delivery, could barely keep up with him even using the shorthand form of note taking he had adopted for just such purposes.

"First, I want every lawyer in the county retained for our position," Proctor told Dillingham. "There was talk again in the *Herald* today about putting the matter to a popular vote. I want to be sure there is no legal representation available for the opposition to try and affect this scheme. It will also give us a great boost with the legislature and demoralize the opposition if we can demonstrate that all of the best legal minds in the county are on our side."

Dillingham shook his head incredulously. "Every lawyer?" he asked Proctor. "You want to retain every lawyer in the county?"

"Every one," Proctor said. "I want every one put on retainer."

"But what if a few have already come out publicly against division?"

"Double their fee. They don't have to do or say anything for division. All I want to do is to put them on retainer and make them unavailable to the opposition and unable to testify for the opposition."

Dillingham raised his eyebrows and inhaled deeply, still incredulous, but said nothing.

Proctor turned toward Frank, then abruptly back to Dillingham.

"Also," he said, remembering something. "All that opposition testimony before the committee—any chance you can get a ruling striking it out?"

"What kind of ruling?" Dillingham asked, a hint of exasperation in his voice.

"What about striking it on the grounds that it is merely cumulative evidence and not rebutting in its character?"

Dillingham chuckled, nodding his head in admiration.

"Brilliant," he said.

Proctor turned back to Frank.

"What about that contract I had you draw up for Ripley? Everything in order? No mistakes?"

"No mistakes," Frank said.

"Draft him a note for $275,000 on my personal account and have it delivered to him tomorrow afternoon. I want it hand delivered."

"Yes, sir."

Proctor turned to Fletcher, who was wetting his lips and wiping his sweaty palms on his pants. He needed a drink badly.

Proctor's influence had helped his son gain the position of secretary of civil and military affairs for Governor Ebenezer Ormsbee, one of Proctor's close political allies. Because of Ormsbee's position, the governor had to remain publicly neutral in the division fight, although Proctor made sure that Ormsbee made every possible resource of the executive office and every pertinent document available to Fletcher.

"Fletcher, what you must get for us from Ormsbee's office is a list of all the Republican members of the House and Senate."

"We already know who they are," Fletcher broke in disdainfully. "What do we need a list for?"

"I don't want just their names," his father replied evenly. "I want a list of each member's personal history. I want to know everything about every single one of them: how many votes they got in the last election, their attendance record in the chamber, who they go to bed with every night. I want to know what they eat for breakfast, who they owe money to, whether they beat their wives, steal from their grandmothers, where their children go to school—everything. I want to know everything about them. If they sneeze, I want to know about it. If they drink, I want to know how much and what brand. If they gamble, I want to know about it. Put as many of Ormsbee's men on it as you have to. We must have it by day after tomorrow evening. We'll meet again then."

"But…" Fletcher began.

"Day after tomorrow evening," his father repeated.

Proctor continued to explain his strategy to the three of them.

"From that list we will proceed, member by member, to determine the exact price of every member's vote. We will twist arms if we have to. We'll blackmail if we have to. Every man has a price. Don't ever let anyone tell you he doesn't have a price. Every man has a price. Some men have a lower price than others, some higher. But we must find the price of each and every Republican vote in the chamber. We will pay whatever price we have to, money, trade votes, whatever it is. We will pay it. But every price must be solid. There must be no second thoughts the day of the vote. We will know before the vote that we will win and we will know by exactly how many votes."

He turned to the boys.

"Frank and Fletcher, you must coordinate this. It is the backbone of our strategy. You will have at your disposal every man from the office you need. Take whatever you want and whatever you need. Offer and pay any price you must. You need not ask my permission. I leave it to your discretion and to your judgment how each member's vote is to be gained."

Frank was scribbling furiously. As soon as Proctor said, 'Frank and Fletcher,' Frank knew the success of the task rested on his shoulders, while the credit would be shared equally. It was a familiar assignment, and Frank did not think twice about it. Already, he was planning ahead.

"And finally, gentlemen…"

Proctor walked over to the fireplace. He folded his arms and turned deliberately to face them. He paused melodramatically.

"I have found the perfect general to lead us into the great battle that lies before us and on to the glorious victory that awaits our cause."

His voice rose with emotion as if he were addressing a detachment of battle-weary soldiers he must inspire to rise above their fatigue and apathy, to forget their tiredness, their hunger and pain and homesickness.

"Tomorrow morning, General William Young Warren Ripley," Proctor spaced the general's name with dramatic flair, "will address the committee with a most eloquent plea, as only he can give, for division."

Proctor stood straight before them.

"With so much honor, gentlemen, and with so much eloquence on our side, we can do no less than succeed!"

Chapter 16

TACTICS

Typically, Fletcher had panicked after his father's instructions to him, Frank and Dillingham.

"Frank," he whined. "How can I possibly get the kind of information Father wants by the day after tomorrow evening?"

Proctor and Dillingham had already left the office for a late-night supper.

"The man's impossible," Fletcher continued, following Frank around the office like a small child trying to get its way with a parent.

"It can't be done. He is just so darn pig headed, he won't admit it. We would be better off to simply withdraw the petitions and submit them again next session. Frank, tell him that what he is asking us to do is impossible. We should withdraw the petitions."

"He wants the information by the day after tomorrow," Frank replied, barely listening. He was moving swiftly around the office, packing papers, scribbling notes.

"Go home and pack a bag," he told Fletcher. "We'll have to leave first thing in the morning."

Frank paused briefly. He straightened, calculating quickly in his head.

"I'll stop by the house and pick you up at 4:30," he told Fletcher, resuming his packing. "That should give us plenty of time to make the 5:05 train for Montpelier tomorrow morning."

"You're as crazy as he is!" Fletcher shot back. "Either that, or you're afraid to stand up to him. I just barely got back from Montpelier! I'm going home to get some sleep. We can take the later train just as easily as the 5:05 train."

"Listen, you fool," Frank came from around his desk where he had been scribbling some notes to the office clerk. "Your father told you what he wanted from us. Now, you can either stay here tonight and get a good night's sleep and face your father in the morning, or you can leave with me in the morning. The choice is yours."

As Fletcher wavered uncertainly, Frank tried a different tactic.

"Fletcher, you really amaze me. This is exactly the kind of scheme I thought you'd jump at. Blackmail, twisting arms. C'mon, it should be fun. That's why your father asked you to take charge. It takes force and a lot of political savvy to find people's weak spot and bring them 'round to our position. You've got both. Your father knew that. I'm only surprised you didn't suggest the scheme yourself, although I'm sure you would have if your father didn't beat you to it. You two really are very much alike."

"The old man can be pretty shrewd," admitted Fletcher, flattered and suddenly interested in the plan as Frank outlined it. "We'll break a few arms, all right. I don't mind telling you there are a couple of members it will give me a lot of pleasure to see squirm. It's a brilliant scheme, and Father was right about giving it to me. I just wish we had some more time, and he wasn't so damn pig headed. I really need a good night's sleep."

"You can sleep on the train," Frank told him.

"Are you kidding? The way that thing shakes and rattles?"

Frank left his list of instructions on the clerk's desk and began packing a large, leather-bound heavy briefcase. Fletcher watched him uncertainly.

"All right," Fletcher finally said. "I'll leave with you on the five o'clock train in the morning. I doubt I'll be able to sleep, but at least I won't have to face Father tomorrow morning with a hangover."

Frank smiled. "Good. Change of plans. Instead of picking you up, I'll meet you at the train station in the morning. Don't be late!" he warned. "We've got a lot of work to do and not much time to do it."

Despite their very obvious differences, Frank and Fletcher really did make a good pair. They complemented one another. As Frank had noted, this was exactly the kind of scheme at which Fletcher excelled. It was also the kind of scheme at which Frank excelled; Proctor just got their parts slightly mixed up.

Fletcher's position as secretary of civil and military affairs in Governor Ormsbee's office gave Proctor and his inner circle almost limitless access to the executive branch. But instead of Fletcher, it was Frank who used the resources of the governor's office to dig and dig and dig to come up with the kind of information about each member that Proctor knew was needed to bargain with each of them. Frank was the detail man; Fletcher the hatchet man. Fletcher took the information Frank gave him and twisted, bullied, bribed, browbeat and blackmailed each member until his vote oozed out of him like water from a sponge.

Of course, Fletcher didn't squeeze all by himself. Proctor blitzed the Capitol with loyalists who also met with wavering members and bargained for votes.

But the biggest fish were always saved for Fletcher who reeled them in brilliantly.

Chapter 17

DEBATE

On November 16, 1886, Judge Luke Poland of Waterville, speaker of the Vermont House of Representatives, opened the debate on the division question by proposing that the recommendation by the legislative committee assigned to investigate whether the town of Rutland should be divided into three smaller towns be ordered to lie and amendments printed to that effect. Members agreed, and two amendments, one calling for the creation of the town of Proctor and one calling for the creation of the town of West Rutland, were adopted by the House without debate. Members took up the Proctor bill first.

But before debate on that measure could begin, Representative Hogan from Rutland proposed a third amendment, namely, that the two acts not go into effect unless each received a majority vote of Rutland voters.

"The argument that Rutland is too big for town government is not true," Hogan told the assembly. "Why, Boston had town government until it had 80,600 people.

"The argument that the town hall is not large enough to hold all of the voters could easily apply to many towns from which no complaints have been heard. It never happens that all the voters are present at town meeting anyway.

"Likewise, the argument that many voters live too far from Rutland also applies equally to many other towns. Besides, the roads in Rutland are good and the people from West Rutland and Proctor can go to town meetings on trains run at the expense of the town.

"Rutland has prospered under its present system of government, and it would be unwise to change it for an uncertainty," Hogan continued. "If the bill passes, Proctor would be under the control of one man and one corporation. Governor Proctor might use power judiciously, but if Governor Proctor should die, the corporation might fall into the hands of men who would not use power so judiciously. Not only that, but if the supply of marble should fail, the town would soon be depleted of its population.

"Mr. Speaker, my fellow legislators, if the present bills are passed, I hope my amendment would prevail. It is simply a matter of justice to the people of the town of Rutland that they be allowed to vote on dividing their town. Members have taken a solemn oath that they will guard the interests of the people of the state, not of one portion only—and in this case, a very small portion.

"Rutland has rights as well as the people of Proctor, and Rutland's rights should be regarded."

Before Hogan could sit down, Knight of Middlebury was on his feet.

"The unfortunate gentleman from Rutland has discussed the merits of the bill incorporating the town of Proctor instead of confining himself to his amendment," Knight told the assembly. "Members are inclined to forget the question before the House."

Knapp stood up. "When other towns have asked to be divided, what has been the practice in regard to submitting the question back to be voted upon by the people of the town? I address my question to members of the committee."

Mansur of Brighton, a member of the legislative committee assigned to investigate the division proposal, stood up to answer for the committee.

"Quite a number of similar questions have come before previous legislatures, and up to the time Burlington asked to be incorporated as a city, this question had never been referred back to the towns for a vote. It is my understanding that such a provision was asked for when Montpelier wished to be divided, but that it became a moot point since the legislature turned down the division request anyway.

"I believe the legislature is the proper tribunal to decide the question and the only one that can do it impartially."

Mansur continued: "Our committee visited Rutland several times and also allowed the opposition an additional week to take more testimony and to prepare a written report. It is my belief that we have fairly and impartially examined all of the questions in this case and have come to a fair and just conclusion.

"Nearly all the friends, as well as the opponents, of the measure agreed that something ought to be done, although the opponents of the measure thought a city charter would be preferable to division. A city charter had been asked for in 1880 and refused.

"The committee was of the opinion that a city charter extending over the whole town should not be granted if it were asked for again. It was our opinion that division was a preferable solution."

Watching from the gallery, Frank heaved a deep sigh and stretched his aching back. He had slept an average of four hours a night for the last two weeks.

Below him, he saw a member struggle to his feet. Frank did not have to check his notes. He knew this was one for their side. He had delivered the payoff—$100, in cash—himself. Frank yawned. The member mumbled his opposition to submitting the division proposals to a popular vote and slouched quickly back into his seat, head down.

Stanton of Roxbury bounded up, eager to show his gratitude for his new committee chairmanship. He glanced triumphantly at Frank.

"It seems to me," Stanton was saying, hands on hips, his waistcost open over his large stomach, "that the class of voters represented by Mr. Hogan as residing in Proctor would not be a proper class of people to refer the question back to for a vote, even if we were to do so.

"I have no doubt that a great many of the people of Rutland are also of the transient class and have no vital interest in the matter."

Hogan was on his feet before Stanton could finish.

"Members of the legislature seem to think that I represent a dangerous element in society simply from the fact that the laboring men elected me by such an overwhelming vote. They seem to infer that we are in a state of anarchy down there," Hogan said.

"But there is no proof that the voters in Rutland are turbulent and that it is necessary to divide them into small detachments. There are not even enough voters in Rutland to make a full brigade.

"And even if there were, *General Ripley*," Hogan shouted the general's name derisively.

"General Ripley," he repeated, "is there and amply able to handle a brigade. And in his absence there remain Colonels Proctor and Veazey to control any defiance of lawful authority."

General commotion erupted in the hall following Hogan's outburst. Speaker Poland gaveled the members quiet.

"I have no doubt that the legislature has the constitutional right to effect a division without referring the matter back to the people," Poland said. "I think it is the better plan to discuss the main question before us before being called upon to vote on the amendment by Mr. Hogan."

Mansur and Hogan agreed that the main question should be discussed without further reference to Hogan's amendment.

Fiske of Morristown then took the floor. "I think one prominent fact, and one which has not been successfully refuted by opponents, should govern in this case—that so large a number of voters cannot successfully transact town business.

"I made up my mind on this matter before talking with anybody simply by looking at a map of the town and seeing the location of Proctor," Fiske continued.

"When I saw how far away Proctor is from the town government, I decided then and there that unless the report of the committee was adverse and gave good reason, I should therefore vote for the bill."

Fiske had made up his mind on the matter after being shown a map of his own farm, thought Frank, *which last week had doubled in size thanks to the note the Morristown bank had written him at Proctor's suggestion.*

Below him, Fiske was still addressing the members. He obviously felt he needed to make sure Proctor knew just *how* grateful he was.

"Everyone can see that the amendment proposed by the member from Rutland is simply designed to give a black eye to the bill," Fiske told the members. "It would be unfair to submit a division asked for by a minority of the voters of the town to a vote of the majority who would be certain to defeat it. Members are here to protect the rights of the minority."

In the gallery, Frank groaned inwardly. *Sit down, sit down,* he thought. *Leave well enough alone.*

But Fiske bulled ahead. Frank could hear him refuting the many charges that had been circulating about the makeup and motives of the committee.

"It has been a fair committee," Fiske finally concluded. "And it has made an honest report."

Finally, he sat down, casting Frank a glance as he took his seat. Frank busied himself with his notebook, ignoring him.

Smith of Vershire got up to say that fair or not, he favored the submission of the question to the voters.

"I would be glad to accommodate Governor Proctor because I admire him," Smith said. "But there comes a time when a man should be prevented from going over to himself.

"The new town of Proctor will have but one industry. Suppose that industry should go down? The town of Vershire had such an experience. It depended on the copper business, which went down partly because of bad management.

"If I could be sure Governor Proctor would live another twenty years, I would vote for the bill. Without such an assurance, I am afraid I must vote against it."

Butterfield of Grafton then rose to say that he favored division.

"Proctor is in two towns (Rutland and Pittsford) as it is now," he said. "It should be a town of its own, and Governor Proctor should be left out of the matter."

Marsh of Woodstock took the floor. "Seeing as how only one previous request ever went back to a vote of the people, I believe the legislature should follow the precedent that has been established and not send the matter back to a vote.

"We should give considerable weight to the committee report. After all, this House appointed them."

"I agree," said Chesmere of Huntington. "Members of the committee did not know previously they were to be appointed. They went down there and did a good and fair job."

Higbee of Charlotte agreed, adding, "The committee was composed of honest men. I, for one, am willing to base my vote on their report."

Kingsley of Salisbury disagreed. "Personally, I'm not convinced by either side. I am quite willing to let the town remain as it is."

Dennison of Pittsford then rose. "The voters of Pittsford, recognizing the situation in Proctor, favor giving up some of their land to form the new town. The population of Proctor is well behaved, and it has good schools."

Then Flagg of Braintree got up and told members, "I favor division."

"I favor division," echoed Goodell of Readsboro.

As member after member rose to voice his support for the Proctor township bill, Frank checked his list. After one member stood up, mumbled his support and quickly sat down, Frank caught his eye and smirked. The member scowled and turned away. Next to the man's name, Frank had scratched, "One mistress, two bastards."

He checked off the member's name on his list. *Cheap vote,* he thought.

Other votes had been more expensive or more ingenious. A West Point appointment for the son of one member, a land swap for another, a committee appointment, an inside stock tip for yet another. Sometimes all it took was a little cash to confirm a member's vote; sometimes just a few blunt warnings about a member's past indiscretions; sometimes just a little political horse trading.

Viall of Dorset finally broke the chorus of support by getting up to voice his opposition to division. Frank yawned. They hadn't even bothered with Viall. He was one of Hogan's men, and Proctor's plan was nothing if not strategic. They had not targeted every member, just the winnable ones, and there were plenty of those without wasting time and effort on unneeded votes.

"The committee members may be honest," Viall was saying, "but they are mistaken. The distance between Proctor and Rutland center, the size of the town hall, are not good reasons to divide the most prosperous town in the state.

"Rutland has not been misgoverned. Its prosperity is evidence of that fact."

After Viall sat down, Speaker Poland hoisted his heavy frame to his feet. Frank saw him and sat up. He knew what was coming and braced himself for it.

"I, too, could not favor division of the most prosperous town in the state without some good reasons. And frankly," Poland said, glancing at Frank in the gallery, "I haven't heard any good reasons for division.

"Six years ago I served as counsel to former governor John B. Page in his attempt to secure a city charter for Rutland. The city charter was advanced because Rutland had outgrown its government. Governor Proctor opposed that argument then, and the bill for a city charter was almost unanimously voted down.

"The situation is not greatly different today from what it was then," Poland said. "To paraphrase Governor Proctor in that debate six years ago, 'I fail to see any good reason for division.'"

Except revenge, Frank thought.

"One problem that threatens our country today is the growth of corporations," Poland continued. "Proctor and West Rutland would both be controlled by a great corporation. It would be worse than the rotten borough system of England."

Bedard of St. Albans said he also opposed division.

Stanton of Roxbury rose. "I can see no danger in this proposal even if Governor Proctor, himself, were to be elected representative of the new town for many years in succession."

Laughter erupted among the members.

Mansur then gave a history of the committee's visit to Rutland.

"The committee spent three days in Rutland examining boundaries and taking testimony," he said. "We held a hearing in Proctor, October 21, in West Rutland, October 22, and spent the evening of October 22, and the morning of October 23 in Rutland.

"In addition, we allowed the opposition one extra week to take more testimony and prepare a written report. Most of the testimony given to the committee in opposition was later stricken from the record under the ruling of the committee that it was merely cumulative evidence and not rebutting in its character."

Frank smiled to himself as Mansur sat down. *What a stroke of genius by Proctor,* he thought, *to come up with that idea for getting the opposition testimony expunged from the record.*

Flagg of Braintree then moved for a vote on the question of incorporating the Town of Proctor. The motion carried, 116 to 23.

Hogan's amendment that the issue be turned back to a vote of the people was taken up. It lost, 134 to 84.

When the question of the incorporation of the town of Proctor came up for a third reading, it carried, 128 to 91.

After the emotional debate and struggle around the Proctor amendment, the proposal to incorporate the town of West Rutland passed almost in silence. The struggle was over. All anyone wanted to do now was go home and forget this awful raw display of power.

"Just because Proctor was incorporated, we should not regard this as a precedent," Poland pleaded with his colleagues before the West Rutland vote, trying to rouse them out of their apathy.

"We have let blood enough," Poland went on. "Before we go further, let the gash heal. We treat West Rutland and Rutland like two warring nations where a wall must be constructed between them. But no such situation exists.

"Just because the town has grown large and prosperous is no reason to divide it."

But by now members were tired of the fight and the rhetoric. The amendment to incorporate West Rutland carried, 112 to 97.

In the senate, a considerably smaller and more harmonious body, the two bills depended largely on the actions of the Rutland County delegation. If the Rutland County members were for it, and Proctor made sure they were, so be it. The other senators were certainly not going to pick a fight with them. If the Rutland County members wanted to carve up the richest town in their county, go right ahead.

On November 16, 1886, the Vermont Senate passed the bill to incorporate the Town of Proctor. The bill incorporating the town of West Rutland passed a day later.

Division accomplished.

Chapter 18

FINAL

Division may have greatly enhanced the political power of Rutland and Redfield Proctor and his fellow Republicans, but in economic terms, it was a disaster.

Division succeeded in permanently beggering what had been the largest and richest town in the state. No taxable marble deposits were left in Rutland. In all, Rutland lost more than four-fifths of its total grand list to the new towns.

Division also legally created on the banks of Sutherland Falls what in practicality had been created some seventeen years before when Proctor first entered the marble business: a company town. Of the 2,163 acres of land in Proctor, worth a total of $6,773, Proctor and the Vermont Marble Company owned all but $462 worth of the town.

But perhaps the crowning gem of arrogance in the whole division battle occurred in the statewide elections of 1888. From the beginning, opponents had cried that the real motive behind division was political, aimed at solidifying and expanding Redfield Proctor's own personal political influence within the state.

Knowing this sentiment, and with opposition to the proposal so widespread, and fearing defeat, Dillingham begged Proctor to publicly assure voters he had no future political ambitions.

"People think you are doing this as some sort of stepping stone to national office," Dillingham told Proctor. "It would help our cause enormously if you were to make some personal assurances about your future ambitions."

"That is not something I am prepared to do," Proctor replied. "I am not going to close out any options for myself or any others. That would be foolish."

“But Redfield, we are in very real danger of losing this thing,” Dillingham told him. “Everyone knows you are behind this proposal. I think it would help if you were to give some kind of public declaration about why this is necessary. You need to tell people that you don’t have any personal stake in this—that you have no higher political ambitions. You are simply doing this for the good of the town, not for yourself or your future political plans. People need to hear that directly from you.”

“You tell them,” Proctor instructed. “I am not going to inject myself personally into this campaign. That’s why I have hired you and the others. You need to tell the members and the people whatever you think they need to hear. If they think we are going to use this as a base to run for higher office, you need to calm those fears and assure them that we have no such ambition. If that’s what it will take, you need to put out the word that I have no plans to run for elective office. Tell them we will also keep out of the campaigns of others should division pass.”

Of course that was not true. Division passed, and so did the promises of politicians.

In the first election campaign after the new towns were created, Redfield Proctor ran unopposed for a seat in the Vermont House of Representatives from the newly created town of Proctor. He was elected by a near unanimous vote and took his seat that year as Proctor’s first duly elected state representative.

Rutland and West Rutland also elected Republicans to the state legislature that year. Rutland, with its two new satellites, was once again solidly Republican with three times the political power it had under the short-lived reign of the Democrats.

Redfield Proctor quickly turned his new power base into a national political force. Also in 1888, he served as a delegate-at-large to the Republican National Convention where he chaired the Vermont delegation.

On every ballot Proctor announced Vermont’s delegation to be unanimous for Benjamin Harrison, the only delegation to consistently cast all of its votes for the Hoosier senator.

“My fellow Republicans,” Proctor announced over and over in his deep, booming baritone, standing in the center of the convention floor.

“Vermont casts all eight of its votes for the next President of the United States, Benjamin Harrison!”

Proctor’s showmanship and unwavering support on every ballot at the convention was instrumental in helping Harrison win the nomination.

President Benjamin Harrison and his cabinet, 1889. *Seated, from left:* Harrison, Windom, Wanamaker, Proctor and Blake. *Standing, from left:* Miller, Noble, Rusk and Tracy. *Courtesy Library of Congress.*

Following his election as president, Harrison rewarded Proctor by naming him secretary of war, only the second Vermonter to serve in a president's cabinet.

Upon his appointment to Harrison's cabinet, Proctor resigned as president of the Vermont Marble Company. He was succeeded as president by his son, Fletcher D. Proctor.

Also in 1888, William P. Dillingham, counsel for Redfield Proctor on the division question, was elected governor of Vermont.

The same year, Proctor's old law partner and pine tar collaborator, Wheelock G. Veazey, who was first appointed to the Vermont Supreme Court in 1879 by then governor Redfield Proctor, was reelected to the high court for a fifth consecutive term. Soon afterward, Proctor used his influence in the new Harrison administration to have Veazey appointed to the Interstate Commerce Commission.

The year, 1888, was not so good for Adolphus Smedburg. True to his word, and following a nearly two-year-long struggle, Proctor finally succeeded in November '88 in removing Smedburg as a trustee of the Vermont Marble Company, entirely breaking his power within the company. Smedburg never returned to Vermont, living out his days in New York, bitter and frustrated.

Frank also moved to Washington in 1889 to become Proctor's private secretary at the War Department. His discreet efficiency and intelligence quickly caught the attention of some of the nation's most powerful and influential leaders.

"Blaine from the State Department paid me a visit this afternoon," Proctor told Frank less than a year after the two of them had taken over the War Department.

Proctor and Secretary of State James G. Blaine of Maine had known each other for many years.

After Blaine's visit to his office, Proctor summoned Frank. As usual, Frank sat down across from him, notebooks and pen in hand.

"Yes," Frank replied, "I saw him on the way out. He gave me a nod. He looked pretty harried."

"Yes, yes." Proctor said, gazing intently at Frank. "He needs some good help over there."

Proctor suddenly shifted position, staring out the window.

"You know when I first met you, you were what, fourteen?"

"Yes, sir."

"I knew even then that you were special, that you were going to have a bright future. I admit I was selfish. I wanted that future to be with us, with me, the marble company, Fletcher."

He looked back at Frank and smiled at him. "You've never disappointed me. You are the most loyal and intelligent young man I have ever met. I trust you completely."

"Thank you, sir." Pleased and embarrassed, Frank looked down at the papers in his lap, reddening slightly.

How wonderful it was to have this man all to himself! Frank thought. *Not to have to share him with Fletcher!*

"Blaine told me the solicitor's job at the State Department is still open," Proctor suddenly said. "He asked me if you might be interested."

"Me?" Frank looked up, startled.

"Yes. It's a great opportunity. It's one of the key positions over there. Blaine thinks you could have a great career ahead of you in the diplomatic corps. There's a tremendous need there for bright, able young men. And Lord knows you've had plenty of diplomatic experience picking up after Fletcher all these years."

Frank could hardly take in all he was hearing, everything Proctor was saying. *So Proctor knew about Fletcher's many lapses! Foreign service! Redfield knew about all of Fletcher's messes he had cleaned up! Travel! The State Department! Solicitor's position!*

Frank couldn't wait to see Fletcher's face. *Foreign lands!*

Frank tried to contain the romantic longing he felt swelling in his chest.

"But sir." His eyes were shining. He frowned, trying to control the emotion he felt taking over his face.

"But sir," he tried again. "The company. You. Fletcher. I couldn't possibly leave your employ."

Yes, how could I possibly leave this man!? Frank thought. *And just when I have him all to myself!*

Proctor was watching Frank's face and inner struggle with amusement. He seemed to read Frank's thoughts.

"You could leave me very easily," Proctor told him. "You have served me, the company, Fletcher, all of us, beyond my wildest expectations. I hate to lose the best private secretary any man could ever hope to have. But solicitor to the State Department! Foreign service!

"Frank, I am not going to selfishly hold you back. You are one of the most able young men of your generation. Promise me you will not make any judgment until you talk to Blaine. Don't close out any options. I learned that a long time ago.

"Besides," Proctor continued, lowering his voice and leaning forward conspiratorially. "It's not like I'll be losing you. I have been talking to Edmunds, the senator from Vermont, about him stepping down early so I could get a leg up on his seat. If I am appointed to fill out his term, it will give me a great advantage in the general election. If everything works out, we will both be in Washington for a very long time. Having you at the State Department would be a great advantage to all of us."

In 1890, Frank left Proctor's employ and moved to the State Department, although he remained one of the Proctor family's closest and most trusted advisors.

In December 1891, as Proctor had intimated to Frank would happen, Vermont senator George Edmunds did, indeed, resign, and Governor Carroll S. Page appointed Proctor to fill out Edmunds's unexpired term.

Proctor was subsequently elected to a full term in 1892, and reelected in 1898 and 1904.

Shortly after Proctor resigned from the War Department, Frank, unable to break his old habit of reading the morning newspapers with an eye for Proctor's interests, brought an article from one of the New York papers to Proctor, who was eating breakfast in his apartment at the Champlain in Washington.

"They are calling your administration at the War Department one of the ablest in the history of the department," Frank told him, handing Proctor the paper folded to the article.

"Really?!" Proctor said, his eyebrows raised as he pushed back his chair and reached for the paper.

"Yes, they credited you with improving the pay and welfare of the enlisted men, reforming a harsh military justice system, cutting the desertion rate by more than half, streamlining the pension process and improving the professionalism of the officers' corps, including implementing a more just promotion system," Frank said, briefly summarizing the article.

"Hmmm," Proctor said, smiling at Frank. "We did all that?"

He began reading the article, nodding in satisfaction. Finally, he put down the paper and looked up at Frank.

"It's about time the common soldier received some recognition for the sacrifices he makes," he said. "All we did was to try to improve their lot and apply some good business practices to the administration of the department. It's too bad we don't have a few more businessmen down here who think like we do."

In 1896, Mary Myers, whose health had begun to fail, moved out of her Washington home to live with her stepdaughter Nellie. Proctor saw her for the last time two years later at a reception in the capital. Proctor had just given the most famous and important speech of his political career.

For a number of weeks, the sensationalist press of the day had reported in shocking detail the many atrocities being committed by the Spanish in Cuba.

In March 1898, Proctor visited Cuba to investigate for himself the situation on the tiny island nation off the coast of Florida. His speech on the Senate floor on March 17, 1898, was one of the most memorable and influential of the era.

"I went to Cuba with a strong conviction that the picture had been overdrawn," Proctor told his Senate colleagues. "I could not believe that out of a population of one million, six hundred thousand, two hundred thousand had died within these Spanish forts...My inquiries were entirely outside of sensational sources...What I saw I cannot tell so that others can see it. It must be seen with one's own eyes to be realized...To me, the strongest appeal is not the barbarity practiced by Weyler, nor the loss of the *Maine*...but the spectacle of a million and a half people, the entire native population of Cuba, struggling for freedom and deliverance from the worst misgovernment of which I ever had knowledge."

Proctor's speech made a huge impression on the nation. He was highly respected by his colleagues in Washington and trusted by conservatives and the business community. His sober account of the misery and plight of the Cuban people greatly increased the prowar sentiment and helped move the country closer to war. Barely a month after his speech, the United States did, indeed, enter into a bloody conflict with Spain.

"Great speech, Redfield," said Senator Charles W. Fairbanks, Republican of Indiana, pumping Proctor's hand enthusiastically. "I do believe you have made the strongest case yet for war with Spain. Well done."

Proctor had just caught sight of Mary across the room. Her hair was almost completely white but still long and thick. She had pulled it loosely back and a few stray wisps fell about her face, softening the obvious lines and fatigue. She was very thin but still erect. Nellie hovered anxiously by her elbow, lightly supporting her arm.

"Thank you, Charles."

Proctor started to move toward Mary, but before he could reach her, Senator Arthur P. Gorman of Maryland, the chairman of the Democratic caucus, blocked his path.

"That was quite a speech, Redfield," Gorman said. "But frankly, I'm not surprised at your prowar report. You would seem to have a personal interest in promoting war."

"What are you talking about?" Proctor asked distractedly, looking again at Mary.

"It's obvious," Gorman replied. "War means casualties and casualties mean marble tombstones."

At his words, Proctor met Mary's eyes in a sudden shared memory. She smiled at him, locked in the same reminisce. He saw her sitting across from him in his old law office, leaning back, laughing.

"The first thing you must learn, Mr. Proctor, is never to say, 'tombstones'!"

Proctor turned abruptly away from Gorman.

"That's preposterous!" he muttered, moving over to Mary. He embraced her gently in greeting.

"How are you, my dear?" he asked quietly.

"Happy, Senator." She smiled up at him. "Now that I have seen you," she squeezed his arm.

"Has it really been almost thirty years since you first walked into my office and changed my life forever?" he asked.

"And you mine?"

She wore a blue silk dress belted at the waist that matched her eyes. She had on black shoes. Around her neck was a double strand of pearls with matching pearl earrings that Proctor had presented her on the occasion of winning election to his first full Senate term.

She pulled slightly away and looked up at him. Her eyes were as clear and blue as ever.

"Senator, your speech was an inspiration," she told him, her hand lightly on his arm. It was shaking.

"Thank you for calling attention to the terrible conditions and suffering of those poor people. We are fortunate to have a man of your wisdom and compassion in the Senate. Because of your speech, I know this country will do the right thing by those poor people." She squeezed his arm again.

"Thank you, my dear," he replied hoarsely, his voice thick with emotion, his eyes brimming. He leaned down to kiss her lightly on the cheek.

"Take care of yourself," she whispered, holding him close.

"Well, well. If it isn't Senator Tombstone," interrupted another of Proctor's Democratic Senate colleagues.

Proctor smiled knowingly at Mary, a last, lingering memory passing between them. He took her hand and squeezed it gently. He straightened and turned to face the other senator who was standing impolitely nearby.

"I'm sorry, my esteemed colleague," Proctor said with elaborate cordiality. "But the correct term is 'monuments.'"

Mary died six months later at Nellie's home outside Washington. She was sixty-nine.

Fletcher, deserted by both his father and Frank, presided over a period of great growth at the marble company, thanks in large part to his father's short leash and enormous influence in Washington.

During the 1890s and into the early years of the new century, annual sales at the company grew to more than $3 million and the work force to more than five thousand.

Marble tombstones at Arlington National Cemetery outside Washington, D.C. Proctor became known as the "Tombstone Senator" for his hawkish views and relentless peddling of his marble business. *iStock Photo.*

So successful was Proctor at promoting his business interests in the nation's capital that marble became the standard construction material for government buildings under both Republican and Democratic administrations long after his death. Ironically, it was not until the administration of another Vermont native, President Calvin Coolidge in the 1920s, that Treasury secretary Andrew Mellon finally put a temporary halt to the use of marble in government buildings in Washington, D.C., on the grounds that it was "too ostentatious" a building material.

In 1906, Fletcher was elected governor of Vermont, the second of four Proctor governors. (Proctor's second son, Redfield Jr., served as Vermont governor from 1923 to 1925, and his grandson, Mortimer Proctor, Fletcher's son, was governor from 1945 to 1947.)

Fletcher's election in 1906 was particularly sweet. He won the Republican gubernatorial nomination that year, the equivalent of winning the general election in those days, over the Proctors' bitter political and business rival, owner of the *Rutland Herald*, and author of the antidivision editorials, Percival W. Clement.

"Revenge is ours!" Fletcher wired his father after winning the Republican nomination. "The best part is, it wasn't even close!"

Typically, Fletcher had misspelled his message, leaving off the last 'e' in revenge. But Proctor was far beyond caring about Fletcher's poor spelling. He smiled with satisfaction.

Redfield Proctor remained an active, vigorous man right up until the last few months of his life.

In May 1907, less than a year before his death, he made his last fishing trip when he took his grandson, Mortimer, to Pico Mountain, Proctor's private hunting and fishing preserve outside Rutland.

"You know your father was never much of one for hunting or fishing," Proctor told his grandson. "He never liked the outdoors much. I was always sorry about that. I feel we missed out on some good times together. I think it would have been good for both of us. I know it would have been good for his health. The outdoors saved my life."

"How's that?" Mortimer answered, glancing at his grandfather.

"You mean when you got tuberculosis in the war?"

"Yes. Walking, hunting, fishing. It all helped me recover. The air here is so clean and fresh."

"Is that why you gave such a large sum to build a tuberculosis sanatorium in Pittsford?" Mortimer asked. "Father just told me you gave $250,000 to build that sanatorium."

"Yes," Proctor nodded. "It's the least I can do. Tuberculosis is becoming more widespread, and Vermont is a natural environment for people to come for recovery. I'm living proof of that."

He cast his line deftly downstream between two low hanging saplings. It plopped gently between them.

"Father said that's the largest individual gift that's ever been given in this state."

"I love this state," Proctor replied, reeling his line slowly back in. "Vermont has been very good to me, our family. When a lot has been given you, a lot is expected in return."

He glanced fondly at Mortimer, who was slowly and methodically reeling in his own line.

"How is your father, anyway?" Proctor said, changing the subject.

"He's always so busy," Mortimer replied. "A couple of weeks ago, he told me a shipment of twenty Poles stayed just two nights and left. Father had paid their passage here, but they thought nothing of breaking their contract. They spoke English well and were dressed in fancy clothes. They told stories about cutters getting ten dollars a day in the city. Two of the single men left with them. It has been the talk of the town."

"What does your father pay cutters now?"

"$4 a day, and $2.20 for polishers."

Proctor nodded. "Yes, labor has always been a problem."

"Did you read about that president of the International Marble Workers Association and how he accused you of running a plantation of white slaves in even worse conditions than the Cubans?"

Proctor sighed and shook his head. "Yes, I saw that. The Cubans did not have a YMCA or a hospital or a library like we have built for our workers. The Cubans did not have a visiting nurse like we provide. Their children did not go to a fine school like the one we built for the children of our workers. The Cubans did not have good clothes and food like our workers can buy in our company store."

"Instead of civic improvements, the union guy said the money should have been put in workers' paychecks so they could spend the money their labor generated as they wish."

"I wonder just how many jobs that fellow has created?" Proctor replied. "He goes around stirring up unrest among the workers, but what is his experience? How many men has he ever put to work?"

He fell silent, lost in thought.

"The company's grown beyond what I could have ever predicted," he resumed.

He looked at Mortimer. "It's all owing to your father and the other young men in charge. One of these days you'll be one of them."

He suddenly interrupted his reverie as he saw Mortimer hook a fish.

"That's it, that's it. Good job," he told his grandson, watching him intently.

Mortimer smiled and frowned as he reeled in the fish cautiously, unsure of himself. He lacked the easy grace and purpose of Redfield, who, even as an old man, handled his rod expertly.

"Let out some more line," Redfield told him. "That's it—easy. Reel him in, let him out. Keep the line taut. Don't break the line. That's it, that's it. Good job," he said as Mortimer finally reeled the exhausted fish in to shore.

Proctor clambered down the bank and waded into the shallows of the river, scooping up the fish in a net.

"That's a beauty," Proctor said, holding the brown speckled trout up as he walked slowly back up the bank.

Mortimer smiled broadly. Proctor was tired and had put his own rod down as he watched his grandson play with the fish. He sat down heavily on a log.

"You'll be eighteen next week," Proctor finally said, glancing fondly at his grandson.

"Yes, sir. May 30th."

Mortimer was busy taking care of the fish and rods.

"It's a momentous occasion," Proctor went on. "You'll be off to college in the fall."

"Yes, sir—Yale. Father wants me to study law, but I don't know."

Proctor nodded. "Yes, I never cared much for the practice of law myself. But it is an excellent preparation for business. Your father says you have done a good job in the office."

"I enjoy the work," Mortimer replied.

"The business has changed so much," Proctor mused. "Vermont has changed so much. The whole country is changing. You know, twenty years ago, I thought I could just stop things from changing by dividing up the town. Did your father ever tell you about that?"

Mortimer chuckled. "Oh, yeah, the great division battle. He was so pleased he beat Percy Clement in the governor's race. He showed me some of the editorials Percy had written about the division. They were vicious!"

Proctor nodded. "Yes, they were. I never should have let Percy get control of the *Herald*. We were in partnership once in the newspaper. Did you know that?"

Mortimer nodded. "Yeah, father said something about that once."

"The press would have been much different if I owned the paper then," Proctor continued. "But we prevailed. The labor element we brought in to work for the company was turning against us. They actually succeeded in electing a Democrat to the House from Rutland for the first time. We had to do something to stop that loss. Divide and conquer. That was my strategy."

"Well, it certainly worked," Mortimer replied. "Rutland, West Rutland, Proctor all are solidly Republican. The whole county is. Our influence is stronger than ever."

"Yes, but I think it is only a matter of time," Proctor replied. "The influx of immigrants from southern and eastern Europe is changing the whole country, its culture, politics, everything. We are somewhat isolated up here."

Proctor gazed around. "But even here, our way of life is changing. Just look at those Poles who went right back. I admit I've been to blame."

He looked somberly at Mortimer.

"But I don't know what else we could have done. We had to bring in outside labor to work the quarries and mills. There was not enough labor here. It was work many native-born Americans did not want to do anyway. We needed cheap labor to keep our margins. Immigrants were the only solution for us. But I can see now that we ended up paying a very big price."

"You're being too hard on yourself," Mortimer said. "Our base is solid. Dividing Rutland was brilliant."

"Was it? I'm not so sure," Proctor replied. "We stopped the erosion and consolidated our power, yes, But for how long? Hopefully, our base will remain solid through your lifetime. But what about your children and grandchildren? It was only a short-term political solution, I can see that now.

"And economically, I think it was very unwise," Proctor went on. "Rutland was booming. It was a grand town, the center of commerce, money, politics, even literary, thanks to Julia Dorr. Why, we had nine passenger trains a day coming into Rutland. Already, Burlington has surpassed us in all those areas. Rutland has declined, I can see that, and I can't see how it will ever rise again."

The men were silent.

"But here," Proctor said suddenly. "Enough of this talk about the past."

He reached into his jacket pocket. "Here is an early birthday present."

"Thank you, Grandpa," Mortimer replied, his face brightening. "What is it?"

"This is the deed to Pico. I hope you will find as much peace and happiness here as I have. Out here, you can really get a perspective on the world. Whatever might be bothering you, it falls away here. I hope you will always remember that your grandfather gave you this mountain because he loved Vermont and the outdoors so much. I hope you will always remember that."

"I will, Grandpa." Mortimer looked down at the papers.

Proctor turned to his grandson, his face sad. "I hope you will not make the same mistake your grandfather made and sell out this spot. Promise me, you will always keep this mountain for outdoor activity."

"I promise, Grandpa," Mortimer replied.

He leaned over, smiling, and touched his grandfather's arm lightly, sealing his promise.

Redfield Proctor. *Courtesy Vermont Historical Society.*

Proctor inhaled deeply. Farther up the stream they saw a deer poke gingerly out of the brush and cautiously approach the water. A chipmunk chattered noisily overhead. The air had a balmy, springtime feel as it gently ruffled their hair. There was a smell of fresh earth, rotting logs and leaves. Above them, the sun glinted through a canopy of thick trees.

"I do believe Vermont is the finest place I have ever been," Proctor mused.

"Yes, it is beautiful," Mortimer agreed.

The two men began packing up their fishing gear. Proctor's face was lined, his beard gray. Even though he had a strong walking stick, he leaned on his grandson as they slowly made their way back down the path.

Epilogue

Redfield Proctor died of pneumonia in Washington, D.C. on March 4, 1908. He was seventy-six.

Fletcher Proctor died on September 27, 1911, after becoming ill in New York City. He was fifty.

Frank Partridge became president of the Vermont Marble Company following Fletcher's death in 1911. In 1930, he was appointed a U.S. senator from Vermont to fill the term of the incumbent who had died. He lost the general election for a full term and returned to Proctor. He died on March 2, 1943, at the age of eighty-one.

About the Author

Linda Goodspeed is a widely published, award-winning writer and author. Her previous book, *Pico, Vermont* (1987, 2002) traces the history and development of alpine skiing in the United States. Goodspeed lives in Rutland, Vermont. For more information about Linda Goodspeed, visit her website at www.lindagoodspeed.com.

Visit us at

www.historypress.net